Soulful Symphonies

JOE ANTHONY

NewDelhi • London

BLUEROSE PUBLISHERS
India | U.K.

Copyright © Joe Anthony 2024

All rights reserved by author. No part of this publication may be reproduced, stored in a retrieval system or transmitted in any form or by any means, electronic, mechanical, photocopying, recording or otherwise, without the prior permission of the author. Although every precaution has been taken to verify the accuracy of the information contained herein, the publisher assumes no responsibility for any errors or omissions. No liability is assumed for damages that may result from the use of information contained within.

BlueRose Publishers takes no responsibility for any damages, losses, or liabilities that may arise from the use or misuse of the information, products, or services provided in this publication.

For permissions requests or inquiries regarding this publication, please contact:

BLUEROSE PUBLISHERS
www.BlueRoseONE.com
info@bluerosepublishers.com
+91 8882 898 898
+4407342408967

ISBN: 978-93-6452-382-0

Cover design: Shivam
Typesetting: Namrata Saini

First Edition: September 2024

Foreword

Mathew Panamkat

A college and University Professor,

A children's author and novelist,

Twice Winner of Best Science Fiction Novel' prize.

I am greatly privileged to have been asked to write the Forward for Poet Joe Anthony's new volume of poetry. Mr. Joe Anthony has two earlier volumes of poetry to his credit. It can be said that he lives and breathes poetry. There's nothing to wonder at this. A person with such extraordinary sensibility views the world around us with different eyes from us, ordinary mortals.

When he opened his eyes and tried to take in the sights and sounds, the first man, Adam, had only the reaction of 'Ooh-Aah', for he could express only his overwhelming feelings.

Let us recall how William Wordsworth felt stifled in the prosaic world of nineteenth-century classicism and went out to the invigorating Lake District of England to breathe some fresh air. It was there that he realized that poetry is a spontaneous outpouring of emotions, while much of classical poetry was bereft of the magic of romance and surprise.

Joe Antony has rightly delved into the mysteries of the mind and its myriad journeys. If his earlier volumes were meditative and ruminative, the present volume of poetry concentrates on the all-pervading theme of love. Love in its various avatars, the good, the bad, and the ugly, and finally, love for our Creator. The title of the new volume is 'SOULFUL SYMPHONIES' which consists of 'A SYMPHONY OF LOVE' and 'A UNIQUE BLEND OF INSPIRATIONAL THEMES'.

Yes, love is the only way, as it is the umbilical cord that unites the entire universe and billions of humans in a fraternal bond. What is Love? To define it is to limit it, says a thinker. However, St Paul's words are apt. *"Love is patient; love is kind. It is not jealous, it is not pompous, it is not inflated, it is not rude, it does not seek its own interests, it is not quick-tempered, it does not brood over injury, it does not rejoice over wrongdoing but rejoices with the truth."* This statement cannot be bettered.

I wish Poet Joe Anthony all success and many eager readers, including me.

Mathew Panamkat

Preface

"Soulful Symphonies" is an anthology of poems which **expresses unbridled emotions, gives free play to fancies and imagination, hits the rock-hard bottom of experiences, and** takes the readers on an extraordinary journey through a pleasurable ambience, where the boundaries between the mortal and celestial realms merge. In this captivating exploration of spirituality, cosmic forces, beliefs, and experiences, the ambiance is forged in the crucible of life, in which we are all tested by the storms that rage around us and we are unable to withstand the relentless winds and biting rain. Readers are immersed in a tale that transcends the ordinary and delves into the mysteries of existence. Poetry has the potential to move our soul or touch our heart, or give us hope and courage to battle onward with our struggles.

The book weaves together elements of mysticism, philosophy, spirituality, human orientation, destiny, and man's relationship with his creator into a homogeneous poetic narrative.

There are two sections. The first is titled A SYMPHONY OF LOVE in which the concept of love in varied shades is examined. The second section 'A UNIQUE BLEND OF INSPIRATIONALTHEMES' analyses life's intricacies in normal and unexpected situations.

Let this book be the crown of your library. Give it a place of honor and take it down from the shelf often. There's precious treasure in it. I hope to hear the sound of the Symphony echoing from the heart of every reader.

Joe Anthony.

About the Author

Joe Anthony had been a teacher of English in reputed schools in Kolkata, Chandigarh and New Delhi in India and in Senior Secondary Schools in the Ministry of Education in Muscat, the Sultanate of Oman. After 40 years of teaching he retired and now lives with his family in Gurgaon, Haryana, India.

Email: joeanthony45@gmail.com

www.joeanthony.co.in

Dedicated

To:

All My Friends

My Well-Wishers

And all readers who find a piece of themselves

within these pages

Contents

SECTION ONE

A. Searching for Love 3
    1. When Love Flowers 6
    2. Like a Maiden 7
    3. Love Blooms in Sacrifice 8
    4. Hidden in Pain 9
    5. Clear as Crystal 10
    6. A Unique Language 11
    7. The Face of Beauty 12
    8. A force that Leads 13
    9. What Matters Most 14
    10. The Essence of Existence 15
    11. Love in Death 16

B. Love's Dwelling Place 17
    1. In the Pure of Heart 20
    2. Love Sways in the Breeze 21
    3. Love Abides in Longing 22
    4. Peep Through Creation 23
    5. Within a Mother 24
    6. Where there's Concern 25

C. Love of a Kind 27
    1. Love with a Price 30
    2. Capricious Love 31
    3. One Way Love 33
    4. Feigned Love 34
    5. Love by Force 35
    6. When Love Isn't Love 36

7.	Love through the Senses	37
8.	Love in Concealed Distrust	38
9.	The Unfaithful	39
10.	The Disconnect	40
11.	Beyond the Senses	41
12.	Self-Love	42
13.	Love is a Fire	43
14.	Selfless Love	44
15.	Filial Love	45
16.	The Most Precious Love	46

D. Experience of Love 47

1.	Love is an Art	50
2.	Her Mysterious Ways	51
3.	Anxious Wait	52
4.	It Keeps No Grudge	53
5.	Confronting Teasers	54
6.	Two Loving Bees	55
7.	The Love Within Her	56
8.	Ravages of Hatred	57
9.	Snobbish Arrogance	59
10.	She Stood Motionless	60

E. Love on a Platter 63

1.	Wonderful You	66
2.	You Were a Welcome Song	67
3.	She Stormed Out	68
4.	You Disappeared	69
5.	Your Elusive Shadow	70
6.	My Futile Search	71
7.	An Accidental Meet	72
8.	Your Eyes Beckoned Me	73
9.	Missing You	74
10.	A New Rainbow	75

SECTION TWO

A. In Empathy's Embrace 77

1. A Welcome Disturbance 80
2. It's Worth the Effort 81
3. Fighting for Justice 82
4. My Brain is a Grave 83
5. A Teardrop 84
6. My Song is Distinct 85
7. The Whirl of Pain 86
8. Forsaken and Forlorn 87
9. Be a Sunbeam 88
10. In the Palm of Pain 89
11. He Confronts the Ordeal 90
12. The Wounded Bird 92
13. Echoes of Spring 93
14. Under His Shelter 94
15. Life without Words 95
16. Secret Seekers 96
17. Waiting Demands Patience 97

B. Winds of Change 99

1. My Life is a Tapestry 102
2. The Abiding Link 103
3. Sorrow and Pain 104
4. Memory 105
5. She Was a Candle 106
6. A Proud Spirit 107
7. A Soul in Pain 108
8. A Genuine Beggar 109
9. A Different Home 110
10. We are Like Circles 111
11. We Love the Morrow 112

12.	An Eerie Setting	114
13.	My Inspiration	115
14.	A Dead Heap	116
15.	We Could Be Their Residue	117
16.	We're in an Evil Era	119
17.	Words are Treasures	121
18.	A Visit to Ajna's School	122
19.	We Hold the Power	123
20.	Suffering and Salvation	124

C. Life Experiences 125

1.	Old Age is Beautiful	128
2.	Today My Heart Died	130
3.	Make Space Within	132
4.	Pilgrims of Hope	133
5.	Blind Performance	134
6.	Change in Strategy	135
7.	Firm Foundation	136
8.	Peace Displaced Turmoil	137
9.	My Cup is Full	138
10.	I Heard his Still Voice	139
11.	A Tragic Birthday	140
12.	A Glass Bottle	141
13.	Plain Truth	142
14.	My Life is an Edifice	143
15.	The Circle Effect	144
16.	A World in Turmoil	145
17.	Swimming in a Cesspool	146
18.	A Treasure Trove	147
19.	The Final Journey	148
20.	Thought- Provoking	150
21.	A Sincere Promise	151
22.	The Normal	152

23.	The Way They Work	153
24.	When Old Age Creeps In	154
25.	An Evil Queen	156
26.	Faulty Approach	157
27.	Overambitious	158
28.	A Master Smuggler	159
29.	The Spider Web	160
30.	The Genocide	162
31.	The Disowned	164
32.	Tranquilly we Lived	166
33.	An Evil Generation	167
34.	For a Good Harvest	168
35.	Revisiting Ajna	169
36.	The Corrupt Lawyer	170
37.	Man's Concept of Law	171

D. In Nature's Bosom 173

1.	Spring Time	176
2.	Beautiful Desert	177
3.	Beneath the Frozen Turf	178
4.	A Romantic Scene	179
5.	A Ripe Old Leaf	180
6.	A Blissful Atmosphere	181
7.	Diffuse the Fragrance	182
8.	In the Arms of Night and Day	183
9.	Her Lonely Home	184
10.	The Mountain River	185
11.	The Sea and The Sky	186
12.	To The End of the Earth	187
13.	The Tyrant Sun	188
14.	The Wintry Wind	189
15.	Rest Before the Quest	190
16.	The Brighter Side	191

17.	Beauty Revealed the Truth	192
18.	Healthy Morning Air	193
19.	The Garden Within	194

E. Penetrate the Enigma 195

1.	She was Different	198
2.	A Mystical Experience	199
3.	An Ancient Manuscript	200
4.	Destiny	201
5.	Invest in Fullness	202
6.	Natural Bonding	203
7.	Crossing the Hurdle	204
8.	Time is aMystery	206
9.	Life in a Granite Chunk	208
10.	Fancy	209
11.	Like The Grain of Wheat	210
12.	Interior Conflict	211
13.	Sterile Outlook	212
14.	Source of Wisdom	213
15.	Beware	214
16.	Time is Dying	215
17.	He Enters Undetected	216
18.	We are his Miracles	217
19.	In a Fancy Mood	218
20.	A Rustic's Query	219
21.	The Womb is a Mystery	220
22.	Get Down to Reality	221

F. Discourse with the Divine 223

1.	God's Spirit	226
2.	To the Upper Room	227
3.	The Call was Loud	228
4.	Lay Your Hands	229
5.	In Expiation	230

6.	In Constant Contact	231
7.	When You are Low	232
8.	Intimate Talk	233
9.	Before a Sacred Icon	234
10.	The Betrayer	235
11.	At His Death	236
12.	The Three O'clock Wonder	237
13.	She Knelt in Prayer	239
14.	Awaiting a Response	240
15.	The Ultimate Sacrifice	241
16.	Joseph the Just	243
17.	Do it Before it's Late	244
18.	Daughter of Phanuel	245
19.	Discard All Add-Ons	246
20.	Women in the Gospels	248
21.	My Guardian Angel	250
22.	Totus Tuus–Totally Yours	251
23.	Silence	252
24.	Generous to a Fault	253
25.	Step into the Sacred Space	254
26.	The God of the Impossible	255
G.	**The Lost Countryside**	**257**
1.	Meeting the Unmet	260
2.	Familiar People	262
3.	Recalling the Past	263
4.	The Village Well	264
5.	Those Village Folks	265
6.	The Old Village No More	266
7.	A Epic Reunion	267

SECTION ONE

A SYMPHONY OF LOVE

SYNOPSIS

Love is the most sublime emotion experienced or expressed by the human heart. It encompasses a range of strong and positive interpersonal fondness and devotion. It is the mysterious force that binds people to those around them and the way people react to situations and events. The symphony of love is a journey of passion.

Love may arise from kinship, personal ties, sexual desire, admiration, common interests and so on. It has infinitely many forms, and it is always evolving and changing in its intensity.

In this third book of poems the author examines how love affects people's values, attitudes and behavior; what aspects of life are governed or modified or even manipulated by the understanding of what love is; how humans respond to various forms of love in situations and with people and the Divine; how this universal language enshrined in the human heart matters in the way people live and act in accordance with the Creator's designs.

Love is beautiful. It can sometimes be ugly too. Love and beauty are twin sides of the same coin. If something is beautiful, one cannot but love it and when one is tired of it one finds it unpleasant or ugly. So it is important to have a true understanding of what love is if its beauty is to be appreciated.

Numerous human activities are results of love or lack of it. It is undeniably the most celebrated emotion of all times and languages. Fierce battles were waged and timeless monuments raised for love. It can build and destroy, touch and transform.

It is more powerful than death. The quest and thirst for love is insatiable. Together let's explore this fiery emotion. May this book be a perfect gift for your loved ones to help them appreciate true love and reject the love that is not.

Hope the reader finds inspiration in these poems.

Joe Anthony

A. Searching for Love

I searched for love desperately
Far and near,
Called out in familiar voices
Loud and clear,
Silence slapped me along the way
Hard to bear,
Refusing to give up I persisted
Didn't fear,
Decided to set an example
Make all aware.

The reply was strong and direct
I was startled,
Search not in the height or depth
I was troubled,
Nor in the red light streets
A place singled,
Search the heart of the genuine
I was thrilled,
Enter the terrain of reality
Hope sparkled.
Flow with the tide of the suffering,
Swim in the sea of the struggling,
Look in the tear filled eyes,
Listen to the orphan's cries,
Peep into the bowl of the beggar,
Walk a mile with the loner,
Watch the posture of the humble,
And the helpless as they stumble,
You'll find love most tender
In all, not in a pretender.

1. When Love Flowers

Love is a flower of exquisite beauty
Blossoming in life's garden,
In times of pain it offers serenity,
Helps to forget the harm done.

Love has colors of mystic nature
Having varied shades,
Its fragrance with celestial feature
On creation it cascades.

Love whispers a gentle blessing
Empowers hearts to glow,
Blends and fuses by warm caressing
And makes units grow.

Like rain love falls uninterrupted
Cooling hearts on fire,
Love's aroma when erupted
Satiates the soul's desire.

2. Like a Maiden

Love is a maiden with soft blue eyes
Peering through the shutter,
Waiting anxiously with deep sighs
For her beloved partner.

The smiling lips on her happy face
Welcomes the weary captain,
Sprinkling him with enticing grace
To give him satisfaction.

When're love walks hand in hand
No pain can hurt ever,
It's an antidote, much in demand,
For one or the other.

Love is the heat of the fire in the hearth
To keep your body warm,
And in turn your soul will find worth
To obtain heaven's form.

3. Love Blooms in Sacrifice

Her pretty face stirred his heart
So did her winsome smile,
Her gestures were clear and vibrant,
Alluring her artless style.

Through his window he slyly observed,
Hiding behind the curtain,
Decided that this girl he deserved
As life partner for certain.

Her voice had a magical flavor
Of which he was enamored,
Her blind eyes were without fervor,
At this shock he stammered.

Both his eyes were healthy and clear,
He felt two were a luxury,
Donated one to his newly found dear,
Hoping a swift recovery.

Her vision was fully restored,
But his second eye lost sight,
To repay his tragic loss she implored
To accept her every right.

Through her eyes he viewed the world,
Sights of sigh and delight
Before their common eyes unfurled
To make them forever unite.

4. Hidden in Pain

Love takes root in sorrow and pain,
In soil that provides an ambiance humane,
Will last a lifetime come what may
For growth and expansion in every way.

Love is nourished and nurtured by tears
Shed during struggles, defeat and fears,
Sterling is their value, none can deny,
Forever we trust and on them rely.

Flimsy and fleeting is the love without pain
Proceeds in divergent directions in vain,
The greater the pain and its duration
The brighter the success of our mission.

Pain truly reflects love's intensity,
Greater love increases pain's severity,
Pain and love modify to make life bloom
For all eternity from the womb to the tomb.

5. Clear as Crystal

Love is a crystal ball with many sides
Each symmetrical in form and face,
Tastefully blending beauty and grace,
Stunning colors, designs besides.

Like crystal it generates positive energy,
Diffuses wherever its brightness glows,
Everyone to itself seductively draws,
Compels them to accept it as a liturgy.

Love's an exquisite spectrum of delight
Elevates and enriches an aesthetic allure,
Mesmerizing variations in texture to ensure
To experience the joy of a seraphic sight.

Love has no border, it's like the eagle,
Transcends mundane or celestial horizon,
Under Its ambit it holds creation
For love isn't final, it has a sequel.

6. A Unique Language

Love is the language of solace
Having a global dimension,
The only tongue that's spoken
Which transcends time and space.

It removes physical barriers,
Withstands the test of trials,
Wins over gently its rivals,
Transforms them to love couriers.

It's the most common linkage
For people to share and excel,
And with inspiration propel
To create their true image.

Love can pleasure ensure
Distilled from ripe feelings,
Creates within yearnings
That's enduring and pure.

Love is the dream in repose
A lullaby to ease your brain,
Serenity and peace maintain
And immense bliss propose.

Love is a pervading brightness
That illuminates your world,
And a path to success unfurled
To lead you to future greatness.

7. The Face of Beauty

Where you find beauty love will abide,
For they're integral, in each other reside,
Couples experience immense pleasure
When beauty's valued a priceless treasure.

You love the beauty of buds and flowers
Compelling are their fragrance and colors,
Such is the magnetic force on couples
Who promote these two despite tussles.

Sunrise and sunset are precious delights
So are nature's marvelous sights,
Beauty external and love internal
Make the perfect match for life eternal.

Creation abounds in love and beauty,
A life devoid of these depicts cruelty,
These are essential to nourish our life
To boost energy in conflict and strife.

8. A Force that Leads

Love is the force to lead us through grief
Into the dawn of freedom and hope,
When hearts are sad and without relief
Love is a remedy with adequate scope.

Look at this candle burning so bright
Sending out a loving smile across,
The stars reflect their love in the night
Blinking ardently in welcome response.

Passing by strangers offers no pleasure
Having had no contact ever before,
Yet their impact is beyond measure
Compelling and impossible to ignore.

A warm embrace of sincere assurance,
A healthy hand shake, sign of agreement,
A candid complement of tender resonance,
Are true expressions of love permanent.

9. What Matters Most

Nothing could ever be stranger
Than a lover wishing his end,
Or save one's love from danger
And live forever with that friend.

Love can saunter through fire,
Plunge into the deep waters,
Scale every scary spire,
It's only love that matters.

Nothing's too hurting or risky,
Keen to die countless times,
Death forges them a unity,
Saves their memory in rhymes.

Death has no sting or venom
It's sweet if the cause is true,
The reward is like the ransom
Offered to be cherished by you.

10. The Essence of Existence

Love is the essence of all existence
Be it physical or metaphysical,
Shadows of love covers all distance
And its motion, endless and mystical.

Love reigns supreme in every heart
Often explicit in a gentle one,
Reserved in exposure and in part
Reveals itself, oft prefers to shun.

Love can gift and promote life
At all occasions, in unknown places,
In times of bliss, in the midst of strife
Wherever is found human traces.

Welcome love as the best of friends,
None can deny its benign feature,
Old age or youth love's force transcends
Making existence by far the sweeter.

11. Love in Death

The harrowing news of his untimely death
Amidst the darkest of causes ever known,
Left her speechless and struggling for breath
Wanting in silence and solitude to mourn.

The flickering candle by her bedside
Seemed to gyrate with her inner turmoil,
For the impact was profound as she sighed,
From such a state anyone would recoil.

Her reaction etched with grief and torment
Engaged in embrace that transcended words,
Reflected that of her friend's intent
And its importance sinking deep inwards.

Transcending the confines of void and space
I breathed a silent prayer and quietly left
Unable to offer them relief or solace,
Pondering deeply at destiny's jest.

B. Love's Dwelling Place

I heard love in the call of birds
In the hum of butterflies and bees
Woodpecker knocking hard on trees
And in animals' unspoken words.

I saw love in people and places
Concealed by events, time and space
Revealed through beauty and disgrace,
And in Nature's diverse faces.

I felt love in the cry of pain,
In the joy of success and reward,
In the touch of a bond restored
And in the cool of the summer rain.

1. In the Pure of Heart

If your love is true and pure
You wouldn't hurt anyone,
But do all the good you can
To see them happy and secure.

If your love is admiration
You won't break a flower,
Nor will you let it wither
But take care with dedication.

If the flower is fragrant and beautiful
You will love and rejoice,
But if ugly when it withers,
It'll be an ordeal, pesky and pitiful.

2. Love Sways in the Breeze

Love came to me like a gentle breeze
Wrapped and left me astounded,
Planted a seed of wonder and ease,
The core of my heart responded.

It then permeated my essence
With vibrant bubbles of thrill,
The feeling of an Invisible presence
Served serenity instil.

Then on I judged everyone I met,
Be they humble or snobs,
With deep love and immense respect
For people of all odd jobs.

Love came easy, I welcomed with grace,
Gladly served out to all,
Love them spread to each unknown place
Aided everyone enthrall.

3. Love Abides in Longing

It's better to yearn and hope
Than to arrive and be satisfied,
The feelings of future joy elope
To maintain your ego gratified.

Far and away at a distance
Neither can meet nor converse
In actual physical alliance,
But through virtual waves.

How far, how long and when
Shall they meet and embrace,
Kiss away the separation,
Be one and distance erase.

Day and night they dream
Longing in passionate urge,
Building up self-esteem
That'll aid each other merge.

Distance is stretched by authority
With conditions for seeking alliance,
Beyond the tenets of morality
Will be considered defiance.

A patient and shrewd approach
Will propel to an agreeable stand,
And help to avoid their reproach
When agreed to their demand.

4. Peep Through Creation

Out of his love God created man,
Gave him the image, His very own,
Lavished upon him beauty and grace,
Settled him safe in an awesome place.

Man had everything he ever desired,
Peace and contentment Eden provided,
But he refused to obey His decree
So the banishment he didn't foresee.

The father gave man a second chance,
Consented to protect him and enhance
His prospect to return with a contrite heart
And obey his injunctions and life restart.

The son descended at the father's wish
Man's body and soul to guard and nourish,
By giving His life to redeem and save,
On souls who repent His seal engrave.

Sin had brought man death and privation,
Jesus saved us by death and resurrection,
The ultimate sacrifice he offered His father
For our salvation, as the ransom donor.

5. Within a Mother

Mother's love is the purest form
Beyond compare and ineffable,
No compromise in quality's norm,
Best of its kind and adorable.

It's unconditional and wholly given,
Resolute, selfless, without bounds,
Pure at heart she loves her children
Like an angel with safety surrounds.

A mother is a candle that melts to light
Her child's world of darkness and fear,
Warms up the freezing feel in the heart,
Provides energy and reasons for cheer.

When a child is annoyed or even sad,
Sick or wounded at heart or mind,
To offer comfort she's always glad,
For her nature is caring and kind.

There's no sacrifice ever too taxing
Nor privations to any extent,
No anguish, regret, pain or suffering
That she wouldn't willingly consent.

Unique and enduring is a mother's love
That can never be measured or learned
Bigger than the ocean or the sky above
Always attentive and highly concerned.

6. Where there's Concern

When you sense chill in your trust
And often know not the reason,
When your love appears frozen
And find no way to adjust,
When your speech turns to whispers
And can't hear another's reply,
Be certain that you promptly apply
The clue your conscience registers.

When the smile of love is a smirk,
And the glimmer of eyes a stare,
When caress turns a creepy affair
That everyone tends to shirk,
When a hug acts like a bench vice
And your movement restricted,
When goodbyes appear labored
It's time for desperate sighs.

                                                        Joe Anthony

C. Love of a Kind

Baffled I was with the result
Of my unending search,
The love was sheer insult
Profane and with a smirch.

I had to pay a price
For a fickle or phony kind,
Select or cast the dice,
For love in senses confined.

Love concealed in deceit
Unfaithful in every sense,
Puffed up with ego and conceit
Adept at artless pretense

1. Love with a Price

For love he paid a price,
Even rolled the dice,
Left his family and friends,
Followed the latest trends,
Tried to conceal his whim
Hoping she'd love him.

She was pleased with the gift,
Flattery was lavish and swift,
Endearments in repeated fits
Stumped and floored his wits,
Little did he suspect
Her intent had no respect.

Soon the taste of the favor
Began to lose its flavor
The initial thrill turned sour
 And began to fade and blur,
Such life wasn't of worth
For deception was from both.

2. Capricious Love

Love is often a floating kite
Having its string detached,
Aimless and helpless in its flight
When no radar's attached.

Love needs motive for any action
Lest lethargy grip,
Rouse it feelers to sense emotion
Should its attention flip.

Memories could be pleasing or glum
That entwine the mind,
Love modifies, makes things wholesome
And keeps them refined.

Love oscillates in diverse directions
Unless there's a guide,
Setting momentum beyond deception
To have truth abide.

Love is a symphony that nature plays
Depending on its mood,
Happy or sad, its melody is always
A delightful interlude.

Love's a mystery over the heart reigns
In all its glory and power,
Wielding its influence on new terrains
Mesmerizing every lover.

Love and dreams are sweet as honey
Both have infinite span,
One has a price, the other is free,
Neither follows a plan.

3. One Way Love

You love someone,
Love most intensely,
And passionately,
How's the return?

You can love one,
Show it by acts,
Mention all facts,
Make it your own.

You can't buy love,
Nor get by force,
It ends in divorce,
A certainty whereof.

Is this the happiness
You always wanted?
From you demanded?
You're in a mess.

4. Feigned Love

Her moonlit face emerged
In my memory lane,
Her zestless eyelids wrenched
My aching heart in twain.

The halo over her head
Like a withering bud,
Cast its gloom and spread
Over me a sweeping flood.

Her smirk had a tinge of scorn
Aimed at causing me pain,
So hurtful like a thorn
Deep within my brain.

The spark of hope grew dim
Doused by her callous spurn,
Her nature cold and grim
Showed no intent to return.

5. Love by Force

Through misty eyes she blinked
Drops of tears followed,
The love that with her linked
Had made her life hallowed.

Now that love abandoned
And left for a distant land,
She could've surely demanded
That he accepted her stand.

Coercive love hasn't value
Nor can such love survive,
Devoid of vital virtue
Its essence cannot thrive.

Love that's sincere and pure
Perseveres to the end,
Stands steadfast and true
Like a dedicated friend.

They say love is blind,
I think love enlightens
Reveals beauty enshrined
Deep within all humans.

True love can help to allay
All concerns of a soul,
Our body, the garment of clay,
Can't protect or console.

6. When Love Isn't Love

Love, your name is Savage Cruelty
Demeaning and vicious in ferocity
When a rival competes to win over
Your affection from your lover.

Love portrays a contorted feature
Cold, unfeeling, fierce in nature,
When a heart is drawn to another
Laws of repulsion come to the fore.

Heartless and savage is love's instinct
To pursue relentlessly the opponent,
When true love is detained and teased
Or in clandestine affairs deceived.

Revenge is the only course of action
When true love in the heat of passion
Decides to treat its new attraction
And hides therein the truth of deception.

7. Love through the Senses

A love expressed through senses
Gratifies your pleasure buds,
Cradled in enticing pretenses
Aroused by your lips and hugs.

A yearning flutters your hearts,
Out of this physical essence,
To a mundane matter imparts
A mystical blissful presence.

Sights and smells energize
Your passive faculties react,
Pleasure sensations mesmerize,
Creating immense impact.

Love is a burning desire
Like fire it can blow wild,
Its unruly hunger misfire
And rudely disperse the allied.

This love in soft skin resides
Sensations gyrate and groan
Makes you feel fuzzy, besides
Leaving you **craving for more.**

8. Love in Concealed Distrust

Simple and chaste were the faces,
Sincere and true,
Of malice or blemish no traces,
In honesty they grew.

They could have lived on for long
With love and devotion,
Had they been loyal and strong
And subdued wild emotion.

He viewed himself a hero,
His self-image untrue,
For most he was a zero,
His colleagues were few.

Their faith was candid and deep
But failed to enforce,
Their attraction took a leap
Headlong into divorce.

She thought she was the light
Beaming with fame,
In pride she took delight
That brought her shame.

The plague that ravaged their heart
Was veiled in deceit,
Suspicion drew them apart,
Their split was complete.

9. The Unfaithful

Like a meteor she swept
Across his narrow horizon,
He was confused and bereft
None came by to enliven.

Felt all courage drained
But wasn't ready to concede,
To axe his dream he strained,
Let painful memories recede.

She had left him alone
Just like a mournful song,
Aloof and alive to groan,
To none on earth belong.

Her thought plagued him much,
He tried to erase her memory,
The tone of her way was such,
A wedge, not a remedy.

10. The Disconnect

She's at the window seat
Surveying the fields retreat,
Mourning o'er her defeat
Due to her friend's deceit.

She left him for his lies,
And for his unlawful ties,
Keeping his romps in disguise
She refused to compromise.

Six months of being together
Ended her invisible tether,
She hoped to find another
Who would regard and love her.

She decided to part ways
And his memory erase,
Embark on a new phase
To live in peace and grace.

11. Beyond the Senses

They saw each other at a dance
Their eyes met and lingered,
They could sense their essence
For love had instantly sprouted.

They never uttered a word,
Their love grew on strong roots,
In silent ways they preferred
To express their love pursuits.

Intimate mainly in emotion
They loved to cherish a oneness,
A bond of mutual devotion
Deep in all its fullness.

A relationship truly profound
Passionate in spirit and mind,
Expressed an affection unbound
Inclined to a platonic kind.

Pining for each other's company
To express their intimate feelings,
On occasions that weren't many
They relished their inner healings.

12. Self-Love

Self-love maintains adverse positions
Positive or negative in value,
It cares only for its own ambitions
Urges all benefits accrue.

Self-love does not settle for less
Demands what it deserves,
Expects self-esteem lavishly bless
And retain all the reserves.

Self-love is a skill by practice learned
For personal growth and cheer,
A trophy with tenacity earned
Living a life austere.

Loving self with none included
Setting standards to dare,
Living solely, everyone excluded,
With no sentiments of care.

Selfish love keeps its own company
With an unreal self-Image
It'll never feel sad or lonely
For it hides the inner urge.

13. Love is a Fire

Love is a mighty fire,
It can warm your hearth
Or burn down your house,
You can never tell.

Do not fall in love,
Everything that falls
Breaks into pieces
And leaves you to regret.

When you feel love
That love surges within,
Intensifies and fills you,
Even chokes you to death.

So play with love
As you play with fire,
Cautious at every move
To retain your essence.

14. Selfless Love

Selfless love is a product of self-love
It's refined with immense care,
It's true concern for the high and low
A virtue we find rare.

Self-care caters to the needs in general
To their health and comfort
It's an ongoing process admirable
To foster positive support.

Selfless love creates magical effects
All around your vicinity
Unlike self-love it blesses and protects
Against all negativity.

An inspiring group of peers around
Prompt unity install,
With vibrant throb of love profound
The glorious past recall.

                                                  Joe Anthony

15. Filial Love

The love of a child for a parent
Is the most positive emotion,
And in this bond it's apparent
It urges regard and affection.

A mother's love has no strings
Is offered lavish and free,
The agape love that brings
Eternal flow of ecstasy.

A mother's heart is the world,
And the heartbeat of her child,
She knows what will unfold
Her response is forever mild.

'Mother' is 'love' in every tongue
A child needn't be taught,
She sees in the eyes of the young
Everything the morrow can report.

Soft like velvet her bosom
To settle a wearisome head,
Her prayer is the final asylum
As she kisses the forehead.

Joe Anthony

16. The Most Precious Love

A love that's precious and tender,
Never ending in splendor,
Steadfast, pure and profound,
Only in God can be found.

His love is gracious and faithful,
Boundless as the sky it's eternal,
Unchanging, caring and forgiving
Is seen in our pain and suffering.

God's love is unfailing and merciful,
His agape love is unconditional,
Despite our sins and failure
And most offensive behavior.

Love is a part of His character,
A salient mark of our protector,
Never will it fade or vanish
For the offer is always lavish.

D. Experience of Love

Searching the heart of love I find
It's a mastered art, a baffling kind,
Keeps no grudge but makes you wait
Teasers intrude and tension create.

Could be tragic when love is lost
Unfeeling despite nature's boast,
Ravages of time playing games,
And arrogance making illegal claims.

1. Love is an Art

Love is an art for some
Who considers it awesome,
Worth, if pursued with skill,
For dreams it can fulfill.

Love can be manipulated
To project some scene related,
To allure a gullible viewer
To become an ardent pursuer.

Love draws singular designs,
Force men keep to the lines,
Pretense is often concealed
And messages temptingly veiled.

But love is life for others,
Most essential for lovers,
It's of celestial essences
Beyond the world of the senses.

There is a beauty that exists,
Unseen yet firmly it persists,
Brings about order and purpose,
For love is life that serves us.

2. Her Mysterious Ways

Torn into shreds my wounded heart
Fluttered in anguished sigh,
Braded a wreath of daring on her part
Before I could die.

Heavy was the weight of struggle and pain
That dragged me down the lane,
Cradling in tenderness she eased the strain
Before I grew insane.

Captive fragrance leaked out and vanished
Leaving an unpleasant smell,
The ambience by her aroma was ravished
Before I could yell.

Hostile emotions floated aimlessly
Through my arteries and veins,
Her giggle altered my mood artlessly
Before I lost my gains.

Her tale is a mystery that opened its lid
To give me a memento,
She penned it on me, I couldn't forbid,
For she kept up the tempo.

3. Anxious Wait

She's at the door anxious and awaiting
Her son's return from service she's praying,
It's been a while he'd gone from her
Had promised to return within a year.

The lamp at the gate burns every night
To guide her son back, to bring her delight,
Months have gone by yet dare not debate
How long should she look out and wait.

The lusterless glow projects sinister shadows
Of branches and leaves whose move she follows
All alone without any friends or neighbors
Her anguished life, a vacuum harbors.

It was after noon, an unexpected hour,
He appeared silently before her door,
Bewildered she collapsed into his arms
The sudden happiness effaced her qualms.

4. It Keeps No Grudge

You may treat love with disgust
Condemn its nature in distrust,
Giving it importance unjust,
But love will always bring trust.

You could pummel its head,
Or complain madly instead,
Deprive its daily bread,
But love's impact will spread.

You may attempt to throttle,
Or fear of danger instill,
Condemn love's agent or kill,
But love will greet you still.

Mercy and pardon are facets
Priced above all other aspects,
They bear love's assets
And diffuse in all respects.

Forgiveness is love's strong point
By the Almighty enjoined,
Someone He will appoint
His love our head anoint.

God is creation's monarch
And love surely is His hallmark,
The light of this divine spark
Will help us heaven embark.

5. Confronting Teasers

She nudges me to advance
Beyond the vacant expanse,
To confront the inevitable,
Though I'm dysfunctional.

Courage and resolve I lack,
Facing ordeals I'm slack,
Her compulsion to proceed
Urges my mind to heed.

Sleeves rolled, with a stern face
I stride hastily in arrogance,
The bullies become nervous
Readily scamper and leave us.

A brave and fearless composure
Creates diffidence and fear
Though they appeared tough
My firmness was enough.

6. Two Loving Bees

Plunged in grief from a secret source
He concealed his wounded soul
In the core of a tulip's bud by force
Deep in the bottom of its bowl.

Hoping his friend would never discover
Even when the bud had bloomed,
But her anxious heart did hover
And found what she'd presumed.

A sparkling droplet left her sad eye
Embalmed his gaping scar,
Her soothing breath was fresh and dry
And could all harm debar.

A ripple rocked his soul and stirred,
A pleasing emotion within,
Was grateful for the love she averred,
Though much to his chagrin.

7. The Love Within Her

The love within her is unearthly
With a touch of divinity,
It bubbles and flows out freely
And affects everyone deeply.

It creates an ambiance replete
With lingering melodies sweet,
In the fullness of the Spirit
That doesn't its flow limit.

Her love is prodigal and rich,
Can empower and enrich,
Its sparks ignite a flame
And gloomy hearts inflame.

Interior is the encounter
Of the aura round her,
In tone, essence or range
Her love does not change.

8. Ravages of Hatred

As the landscape of her life she views
Painful memories are let loose,
Like a scarecrow alone she stands
Spreading fear in all the lands.

Once a wholesome scene serene,
Its virgin beauty now obscene,
Ravaged by undue hatred and greed
As warring tribes had refused to concede.

Far and wide in every direction
Pillage and slaughter without discretion
Altered the ethos of a land pristine
Caused a people's value decline.

An alien façade has been projected
Replete with ghastly images injected
That doesn't evoke any pleasing emotion
But leaves a sense of value erosion.

A bashful exterior devoid of gleam
Portrays the essence of a long lost dream,
Eyes like knives can pierce and slice
Even stony hearts with such device.

Rarely a flower is seen to bloom
That can alter the existing gloom,
Against a backdrop of bruise and blemish
It can't nectar or fragrance furnish.

Here the breeze has deadly stings
Never a soothing caress it brings,
Birds in depressed monotone warble
About destruction and pain in battle.

Her wounded heart she conceals in secret
Silently bearing all pain and regret,
Bleak is the hope for a life to restart
In this blood soaked field torn apart.

9. Snobbish Arrogance

Bathed in cold sweat she stared
At his abrupt appearance,
He had left her uncared
Posing a snobbish arrogance.

A tapestry of emotions assailed
And harrowed her bleeding heart,
Myriads of feelings prevailed
To ignore his advance to restart.

All his enticements failed
Strong were the barriers she built,
Seeing all options derailed
He took off consumed by guilt.

Wavering isn't a solution,
Escapism only an illusion,
Face the challenging rival
It's the best way for survival.

10. She Stood Motionless

Standing at the threshold none to console
Scanning a void dark and foreboding
She stood motionless like a lost soul
Seeing nothing yet grasping everything.

Teardrops turned into cascading streams
On a virgin face unused to affront,
Colorless fusion of hazy day dreams
Sprayed in abundance wanting to confront.

A disaster can alter the value of matter,
A photo long discarded can turn adorable,
An ignored tomb can be a saint's altar,
A rejected object, a relic most valuable.

She left the threshold for the tragic scene
Hoping to find meaning for her existence,
She could only see a white blurry screen
With her image emerging at a distance.

Though thoughts ebony, her need she shares
Donning the purple garment of sorrow,
Her cherished dreams have turned nightmares
Forecasting a shadow of uncertain morrow.

Despair and confusion gather momentum
Constraining courage to bring up the rear,
Leaping and skipping in relentless tantrum
Blind to the lurking viper of fear.

Cradling her head in her rugged hands
She empties her mind and bares her heart,
Heaven seemed receptive to her demands
The glow in the sky augured a restart.

Joe Anthony

E. Love on a Platter

She came to my life with a smiling face
Like a melodious tune that didn't last,
Left me bone dry and cold at the start
So I decided her impression erase.

Her elusive shadow traversed my road
Compelling me to make a futile hunt,
I could approach her in joy or confront
Fortune favored and love was bestowed.

Two uncertain eyes beckoned me closer
Hinting that we could unite as one,
In this sudden surge I was outrun
My spirit went numb at this poser.

Life took a sudden and unforeseen turn
Altered all manner, demeanor and mode,
A world of beauty and peace soon followed
In my heart the flame of love began to burn.

1. Wonderful You

Your face projects the essence of grace,
A gracious quality divine,
Your loving embrace can sorrow erase
 And for us comfort define.

Your brow is an altar, your head a shrine,
In the edifice, your body,
All your faculties in unison align
To form you a holy entity.

Your breath is a soothing balm to the mind
That sorely needs a revival,
Your whisper is a Psalm the fingers find
To string their urge for survival.

Your lips vibrant whenever you smile
Are enchanting for sure,
Your sparkling eyes reflect no guile
Instead they support assure.

Upon your being is innocence engraved,
A distinct angelic mark,
You are a creation saved and revered,
Heaven's hallowed monarch.

2. You Were a Welcome Song

You came to me like a song
Swaying in the evening breeze,
Cool was your touch to prolong
The pleasure of comfort and ease.

Your breath caressed my face
My heart flushed with delight,
The throbbing in your embrace
Kept me awake all night.

Your lips touched my eyes
Wet with tears of bliss,
You heard my unrestrained sighs
At your tender kiss.

We sang and danced all night,
Talked of future designs,
Life seemed to blossom bright
Grateful were we for these signs.

3. She Stormed Out

Reclining on the garden swing,
Where we often lazed,
Beautiful moments recalling
That had kept us amazed.

We ate and drank in abandon,
Talked and sang with zest,
Lived our love with passion
For we had all the best.

We yelled at each other often,
Argued and quarreled at times,
But we maintained caution
Didn't commit grave crimes.

One night you behaved puerile
Stormed out in violent fashion,
My persuasion proved futile,
I still don't know the reason.

4. You Disappeared

You left me without a warning
I failed to fathom the reason,
Dug up my mind for treason
That could've forced your leaving.

I searched in total despair
Within and beyond our dwelling,
All our friends I kept calling
None of them seemed to care.

Anxiously long I waited
Hoping you would return,
You'd been full of concern
I felt utterly wasted.

To be life partners we'd vowed
To cooperate with each other,
Through thick and thin together
We lived so long and loved.

5. Your Elusive Shadow

Often I see your elusive shadow
Spreading over this expansive meadow,
Fading gently I watch it approach
But vanishes each time I try to reach.

In whisper soft your shadow echoes
The stifling breath of your spiteful foes,
I can't hear or grasp its message
Have no talent to decode its presage.

The faint tone of your melody's cadence,
Like the repeat of a chorus in abeyance,
Resonates within the recess of memories
And soon my mind is lost in reveries.

Musings wet with teardrops of pain,
Despite our struggle to erase all strain,
Throbs afresh my love-eaten heart
Searching for meaning in life to impart.

The waves of thoughts are weak and weary,
Unknown to the shore they lash in fury,
The lonely evenings in mournful silence
I wait anxiously for comfort and guidance.

6. My Futile Search

Bereft of losing you, my partner,
Devastated at your leaving,
Devoid of dignity and honor
Nothing seemed any more appealing.

Lost in the desert of solitude,
Marked by silence and void,
Guilt began in earnest intrude
I felt my life being destroyed.

You left no evidence behind
That could have aided my search,
You didn't want me to find
So you left me in the lurch.

I walked on burning ember,
Dived into frozen water,
Frequently lost my temper,
Future didn't seem to matter.

You have vanished from sight
But my feelings won't lessen,
I shall still watch and wait
Sometimes strange things happen.

7. An Accidental Meet

Years of darkness drifted
Over my cloudy sky,
Female circles I resisted
On them I couldn't rely.

Passing through a boulevard
A familiar face appeared,
Her laughter smote me hard,
Wasn't that smile I'd revered?

She clung to someone's arm
And swayed like a wanton,
Her eyes had a look of alarm
For I seemed a friendly one.

She saw me and hid her face
Ashamed to confront the truth
Guilt stifled her voice
Her reactions were uncouth.

I observed her strange conduct,
Anxious and greatly unnerved,
Her qualms created distrust
All contacts were severed.

I hated the wound reopen
Though dried, had left a scar,
Deep in my heart as a token
Of a life of love gone bizarre.

8. Your Eyes Beckoned Me

As I gravitate to your avenues of grace
The barriers fall away giving me space,
Drawn into that circle of love in place
An infinite volume of thrill I trace.

Your twinkling eyes like a fishing hook
Lured me into that fated nook,
Ensued that the bait I took,
To let me walk away you didn't brook.

Whatever you performed outwardly
Somehow it dawned on me inwardly,
Like the neon light glowing timidly
Beside the one shining more brilliantly.

This love ensured an intimate union
Replaced every other likely illusion,
Like through pain when healing is won
There evolved a perfect fusion.

9. Missing You

Your memory's like a misty shadow,
Each time I decide your trail to follow
It grows faint and vanishes from sight
Leaving my spirit in an unhappy plight.

I hear your silence in the drizzling haze,
Follow your outline with straining eyes,
Like the lost effects of a favorite song
That has haunted my memory for long.

My blurred eyes scan your life's pages
Of souvenirs wrapped in teary urges,
Search vainly for meaning in distance
Created between us by heaven's instance.

My waves, weary of thoughts very lonely,
Adorn my life's shore crying silently,
Upon me falls your whispering breath
And stirs passionately my soul's depth.

By the tranquil twilight longingly I wait
Staring far for a glimpse of my soul-mate,
Like the burning pain when memory fades
Leaving me distraught as despair invades.

10. A New Rainbow

You opened afresh a new chapter
With sunshine and radiant rays,
A rainbow to thrill me with rapture
And set my heart ablaze.

You unlocked a world of beauty,
Revealed a wondrous amalgam
Of values of superb quality
To prevent me to vice succumb.

The thrill of an ardent moment
Shared with you is a bounty,
Let this wine of love ferment
To savor and share with many.

All that's pretty and precious
That's deep within me at rest,
I pledge you this offer gracious
And gladly in you invest.

I'll seek neither fortune nor fame,
Nor pleasures of any kind,
With you gladly I'll share my name,
Have our avowal signed.

Joe Anthony

SECTION TWO

A UNIQUE BLEND OF INSPIRATIONAL THEMES

A. In Empathy's Embrace

We could term empathy as the ability to sense other people's emotions, together with the skill to imagine what someone else might be thinking or to understand, feel, and possibly share and respond to their experience.

Empathy and compassion are close synonyms. Compassion is characterized by the desire to take action to help the other person while empathy is in action.

1. A Welcome Disturbance

The fingers of rain played on my window
Waking me before time,
A flurry of breeze then entered on tip-toe
Making my feelings sublime.

Genial sun shafts warm and refreshing
Permeate through every pore,
Floral fragrance gently caressing
My whole being to the core.

Gliding in stillness fancies pervade
Wrapping me in their arms,
Whispering dreams my soul invade
Binding me in hidden charms.

Lost in oblivion I fell into slumber
Moved by a force unknown,
The open window showed no finger
I was glad to be alone.

2. It's Worth the Effort

If you can enter pain and sorrow
Permeate their every part,
If you can emerge with trust on the morrow
Vanquish hatred from the heart,
The bleak winter shall bloom in color
Provide a pleasant summer.

If your neighbor's dog wakes you at midnight
Wild with alarming bark,
If your car breaks down at a traffic light
Helpless to move it to park,
Patient approach will alter the case
And all anxiety erase.

If you inhaled the toxic air
With high content of venom,
If the food delivered at your order
In time didn't come,
Grievance cell can assist in the matter
Solve the problem faster.

If your teenager or any elder
Throws an unhealthy tantrum,
If the plans you made to live in splendor
Got derailed at random,
Change your ways to match the objective
You'll find life effective.

3. Fighting for Justice

The venom of hatred blazed in her eyes
Hotter than the magma any barrier defies
Stretched the distance twixt truth and lies
Lashed the patrons who sought compromise.

The sword she drew to confront the foe
Sliced their intent with a mighty blow,
Fought for justice and peace to bestow,
Disgrace and shame brought them misery and woe.

Like the hostile waves slap away sand
In raging words she roared her demand,
Her fierce onslaught unable to withstand
Defamed, they were forced to disband.

4. My Brain is a Grave

My humble brain is an enormous grave
Interred therein are the elite brave,
The smart, the pretty, the tall and the rich,
Each of who obtained a unique niche.

Souls in rapture with lilting eyes,
Vibrant hearts with soothing sighs,
Thoughts and feelings, abiding stories,
All rest in comfort with fond memories.

Corpses of cowards and flawed are buried
With the ugly, wicked, dull and wearied,
A level beneath this privileged layer
Lie those who received lesser favor.

Those lived in pain, distress and fears
Tethered to defeat and blistered by tears,
Beside them rest those less favored
And every unknown along with the wayward.

5. A Teardrop

There's a teardrop at the eyelids' edge,
To hold or drip it I dither to judge,
I could wipe and dry my eyes
And its fall could relieve my sighs.

Holding on is against my nature
Could generate a hurt much greater,
Releasing it would ease the tension
And assist to focus on my vision.

Blurred eyes present a sight unreal
What appears is rather surreal,
Clear the eyes for correct perception
Avoid the danger of visual deception.

6. My Song is Distinct

My song has thoughts and feelings
Of love and concern,
No place for words and dealings
But power to discern.

Mellow the tune to the listener
It soothes the mind,
In the throes of tension and fear
Comfort you'll find.

Extreme is the joy that unfurls
From deep gashes,
In colors and sounds it swirls
As hope flashes.

Come then listen to its echo
That throbs your heart,
Let what's futile forgo
And happiness impart.

7. The Whirl of Pain

Pain is deeply a traumatic feeling
Seeping up your spine,
Often intense and loud in telling
It's difficult to define.

Pangs of pain comes in varied forms
Moves in slithering waves,
Mild or violent it always deforms
Makes your senses slaves.

Physical pain when intense and piercing
Can drive you awfully wild,
Emotional agony is severe and stinging
And is denounced and reviled.

Pain in general can be therapeutic
For your body and soul,
Sublimating pain can be like music
And bring things under control.

8. Forsaken and Forlorn

Forsaken and forlorn she roamed the street
Unwanted and unloved on deformed feet,
With empty stomach and nothing to eat
Hoping for someone to give her a treat.

Beneath a bridge she found shelter from rain
But the bed she made only brought pain
The stone for a pillow was all in vain
For sleep decided its distance maintain.

She had a worn sheet to wrap her frame
In the freezing wind a sleet it became,
After a night of protest and blame
She stepped out into a day of shame.

One more day to scavenge for food,
Tolerance, approval and love she pursued,
Not truly knowing if that was she should
For always such as these seemed to elude.

9. Be a Sunbeam

I'm a sunbeam peering at a bleak world
Lighting an ambiance dark and cold,
Providing energy and warmth for free
Offering these with absolute guarantee.

You'll find me peeping through squalid hovels,
Purging the filth at all neglected levels,
Filling beggar's bowls with startling surprises,
Warmth and zest to urchins in crises.

I spread joy in the huts of the oppressed,
And spray smile on the unduly depressed,
All my brightness and unflinching ardor
Transform what I touch with sincere candor.

A sunbeam is meant to create energy,
Provide means to stave of lethargy,
Evoke and retain vigor and vitality,
Bring about content based on reality.

10. In the Palm of Pain

Cocooned I lay in the palm of pain
Writhing in restless agony severe,
Hoping for a caress soft and humane
Like a mother's whisper in my ear.

Turbulent signals flood my brain
Lash about in violent throbs unknown,
Enter brutally my heart's domain
Crushing me as I struggle and moan.

Pain was a blade that sliced my skin
Flaying my entire body and mind,
Killing by torture the life within
As my feeble spirit moaned and whined.

The palm of pain closed tight and squeezed
I thought the end had at last arrived,
When the palm opened I felt released
The pressure exerted got me revived.

11. He Confronts the Ordeal

A mystic ordeal with the taste of pain
Flowed on his palate of despair again,
Suffering's a mission God has ordained,
A grueling means to purge the stained.

A strange emotion, fierce and intense
Erupted in explosion with a force immense.
Jolting, rattling and swaying his frame
Bewildered, he plunged deep into shame.

On bended knees at heaven he knocks,
Ego and pride were his stumbling blocks,
His conscience had a double sided visage
That reflected his ego and God's image.

A giant leap is the hinge point change
For slumber and oblivion to bridge the range,
So he exits the hostile ambience
And rises to a realm to refine his essence.

Like a tiny bud afraid to bloom
His effort reflects an insipid gloom,
He strains his mind to suppress the emotion
That restrains him from applying reason.

In trance he hears a familiar strain
That provokes a stirring within his brain,
Nature must succumb to grace, he decides,
A strenuous tussle the result provides.

The Lord winnows the heaped up grain
To remove the chaff, the wheat's stain,
So, firm in resolve he emerges in faith
Submits to the Lord in grace to bathe.

12. The Wounded Bird

She held the tiny bird
That fell from its nest,
In her hand stirred
Its soft pulsing breast.

Afraid to hold it tight
Cupped it in her palm,
It could die of fright
Or cause the wings harm.

She kissed its open beak,
Breathed into its ears,
Patted its body sleek,
Whispered to allay fears.

Soon back to normal
Had a sip of water
Pecked at the morsel
Took off, didn't falter.

13. Echoes of Spring

Buds and flowers are witnessing
Butterflies gaily dancing,
Drawing halos unceasing,
And in heaven's name blessing.

Honey bees humming melodies
Charming the vernal prairies,
Relaxed and lost in reveries
I lay lost in memories.

The wind spoke a language
From a point of vantage
With an enigmatic tinge
Providing me with leverage.

Hands joined in prayer
Refusing to give in to despair,
Pleading heaven to spare
In peace I slept unaware.

14. Under His Shelter

Like the sparrow that found a shelter
And built its nest below the altar,
Housed its nestlings in safety and solace
I too was blessed with a congenial surface.

Cradled in the warm and gentle hands
Of the only one who understands,
Though feeble, frail and weak I be,
I can now observe and things foresee.

There's no frontier I can't cross,
Nor any ocean I can't cruise,
Not a mountain I can't scale,
Because I have the Divine seal.

I had lived through complex times
And had committed untold crimes,
Feared to raise my wings to fly
Thought my weight wouldn't comply.

From a mundane stage he launched me
Into his treasure house to be a trustee,
Unlike the sparrow, that little bird,
Now within me an eagle stirred.

15. Life without Words

People communicate without words
Though strange it may sound and queer,
Sounds released through vocal chords
Can convey messages equally clear.

Sadness is conveyed by sighs and cries
Much is revealed by the glance of eyes,
Heart beat can create joy and cheers,
Silence transmits message to the ears.

Gestures are signals of thoughts profound
More forceful than word or sound,
Furrowing brows expose negative emotion,
Smiles and laughter speak for the unspoken.

The fewer the words the lesser the harm,
Keeping distance is no cause for alarm,
Without words they lived in the past,
Is our life then better in contrast?

16. Secret Seekers

Woven complex webs of concepts
About the life of the human soul,
Shrouded in mystery that upsets
And sends such seekers out of control.

In the book of life what is written
In its essence is hard to fathom,
From common man it is hidden
Sharp wits can sense it at random.

The search may lead you even to despair
As you find no hint or suggestion
Humbly consult an erudite doctor
There's a way to achieve your mission.

17. Waiting Demands Patience

Waiting is a life changing experience
Especially waiting on God to respond,
Often we hear only his silence
Though be close to us or far beyond.

God knows you're tired and are in need
Don't give up, await and keep marking time,
His voice is everything we need to heed
To lead us to the land of happiness sublime.

He often does his work behind the scene,
His delays couldn't mean his denials,
For that seems his normal routine
It's his way of testing us with trials.

God may be silent but he's in place,
His time is perfect we can't deny,
His clock ticks at a distinct pace,
We only need to trust and comply.

Joe Anthony

B. Winds of Change

Change is observed in all forms and aspects of life. Some changes are external and can be easily noticed. Others are internal, spiritual or emotional, and can be discerned only by careful examination. Change is essential but it should always be for the better and should be progressive.

Change is effected by innumerable agents. Wind is one of them. It comes and goes bringing about change, some beneficial, others harmful. When we accept the effects of change we experience transformation.

1. My Life is a Tapestry

My life is a tapestry of exquisite value
On a fabric with marvels ancient and new,
Weaving the warp and weft of my actions
A timeless expression that portrays my visions.

It's woven by God with his creative hands
With colors merging on symbolic strands,
Making me a product of brilliance and worth,
A kaleidoscope of existence given rebirth.

All joyful images that in him abide
He needles skilfully on my upper-side,
But on the under-side sad events he keeps
That the whole fabric his nature speaks.

Seams and tangles at hem joint pleat
He fashions and molds with beauty replete,
A tapestry of wonder you'd love to own
And transform your home into a celestial zone.

2. The Abiding Link

Old Age is sadly settled in hurts
In the attic of its cottage,
Grey hair masked by the frost of age
Symbolic of its efforts.

Below struts Manhood in all its vigor
Living a life of comfort,
Revealing tangibly his wealthy state
Unaware of the other.

Under the shadow that sweeps over
Stumbles Youth jubilant,
With the flush of energy flamboyant,
Manifests its power.

Last in line crawls the Little Infant
First to begin the link.
Its lively eyes can speak and think
A quality inherent.

The wind sings in the ear of the Child
On Youth the sun smiles,
In love and devotion Manhood beguiles
And Old Age is always mild.

3. Sorrow and Pain

Like moonbeams piercing the dark cloud
To clear a path for the stars to shine,
Heaven's bolt strikes at our pain aloud
To split it into pieces and refine.

We may fail to see the light
Due to its dazzle blinding our eyes,
Like when sorrow bars our sight
Our heart contrite pleads and cries.

Beyond the shadows of doubts and fears
The moon of love will casts its shine,
No sorrow or pain shall emit tears
But their amalgam love shall enshrine.

When we arrive at heaven's portal
We'll know why the cloud was dark,
Why the moon beam, though only mortal,
Would be the vessel we were to embark.

4. Memory

Memory's a tree rooted firmly
Within the ambit of reason,
With will and desire working formally
Like in a normal person.

Its rustling leaves of interaction,
With fancy and creative power,
Adorn the stem of fascination
To produce the expected flower.

Luscious fruits of appeal and passion
Add some flavor of insight,
Dangling on branches of inspiration
Drawn from the mind of an artist.

Nourished by sunbeams of creativity
Nurtured by the ever inventive skill,
Vitalized by the passion of curiosity
Memory can empower, values instill.

5. She Was a Candle

She was a candle at the altar
Tall and upright,
Melted but didn't falter
As she burnt bright.

Slim was the flame that lilted
As the choir sang,
In unison their voice uplifted
The faithful's pang.

Her glow and prayerful gait,
Awesome and inspiring,
Was a source of joy to relate
And worth admiring.

Dressed in vestal brightness,
Her soul diffused
Heaven's innocent fineness
On the seduced.

Her look focused heavenward
In ecstatic grace,
She never uttered a word
But all were ablaze.

6. A Proud Spirit

Our spirit shouldn't be proud
Hiding in a vanishing shroud,
Vane and ignoble by nature
Needn't promote it or nurture.

The boast of the spirit be noble,
Its dealings in all respects moral,
Blessed with heavenly life force
The mundane can't be its course.

The grave will never be prison
That can conceal its vision,
Matter and form must decay,
The spirit will forever stay.

With essence calm and benign
The spirit with heaven must align,
To dwell in a celestial shrine
Fashioned by the Lord Divine.

7. A Soul in Pain

I heard the cry of a person in pain
Slicing the silence of the earth's domain,
Tearing apart in anguish insane
Cherished feelings she wished to retain.

No help appeared to relieve her mind
Nor any consolation could she find,
All the unhappiness she'd left behind
Reared up again to keep her confined.

Unable to fathom the depth of the loss
She would face from her recent divorce,
Felt compelled by a mysterious force
A turbulent river she'd wade across.

The waves were savage in fury and flow
She couldn't withstand their persistent blow,
The onslaught so severe she didn't know
Was sucked into a chasm that yawned below.

8. A Genuine Beggar

He hasn't assumed a beggar's poise,
Though truly one, it wasn't his choice,
Roaming the streets in discarded rags
Like a kingpin of rebellious gangs.

Pleading for alms with extended arms
Holding a bowl out, he has no qualms,
Head bending low in an act servile
Veiling the sense of shame all the while.

Being despised in hostile temper
Fanning to flame every resentful ember,
His dejected heart revolts in anguish
His body and mind like prisoners languish.

Aggrieved sentiments arise in revolt,
Conscience poses a constant assault,
Crushed under pressure unable to resist
Hopes anxiously someone will assist.

Life can't linger on this slippery road,
He needs to come by a job and abode,
Hoping for a chance to restart his ways
Awaits in patience, to heaven he prays.

9. A Different Home

He left me abruptly at the gate,
They took me in, didn't hesitate,
I watched him drive away in haste
His attitude made me irate.

The nursing home welcomed me,
I felt abandoned but free,
Just yet another entity,
No future I could foresee.

My man showed no remorse
Though it was done by force,
She insisted he should endorse
And made my life morose.

I complained of utter neglect,
Remember how often I wept,
It wasn't easy to forget
My own showing no respect.

When viewing the golden tinge
That pierce the summit's fringe,
I brood in sadness and cringe
But I didn't consider revenge.

Out of solitude and grief
Often emerges relief,
So holding on to my belief
That my stay here be brief.

10. We are Like Circles

We are like circles in water
In the flux of waves,
In ripples we alter
The way our orbit behaves.

The verge forever expands,
Engulfs the shore,
Shuffling the sands
Back to order restore.

Steadily we make advance
Against all conflicts,
Our efforts enhance
The quality of the results.

11. We Love the Morrow

Tomorrow's a favorite word
To which many people adhere,
Its touch is weird or absurd
Its grip on men is severe.

It's before you with assurance
That you are certain to arrive,
But you don't get the clearance
However desperate you strive.

You may send an invite
It never arrives, they say,
All your influence despite
Your efforts end in dismay.

Tomorrow brightens your eyes
Change the color of your thought,
Adds beauty and glamour to lies,
But intransigent in support.

Tomorrow can produce wings
Become a fairy and fly,
It's just a dream that stings,
In anxiety you can only sigh.

The timeless echoes of attraction
Charged with wonder and intrigue,
Is tomorrow's societal seduction,
To create anguish and fatigue.

Permit not tomorrow govern
Ignore its displayed result
All your endeavors summon
In content you will exult.

12. An Eerie Setting

I hear the willow wailing in agony
Waving its branches in manner uncanny,
Nobody seemed to fathom the mystery,
The wailing brought about unending misery.

Birds in haste abandoned their nets,
Desolate sighs echoed only regrets,
No form of existence dared to remain,
Eerie indeed was the state of the terrain.

Wolves were heard to howl in the night,
Lonely and dark the scene was quiet,
Moon light smeared an unholy hue
Portraying a scene of appalling view.

Night dissolved into a bright sane day
Eclipsing the evil that brought dismay,
Zest and hope in abundance loomed,
The willow emerged fresh and bloomed.

13. My Inspiration

I pursued her steps close behind
Along the path she ardently designed,
With curves and loops on even ground
To make my experience truly profound.

People with whom she interacted
Or whose lives most impacted
Always received interior guidance,
As I did when we were in alliance.

I wrap my arms around this mystery
Into the very depth, not the periphery,
Being a part of her entire picture
I long to imbibe her angelic nature.

When crops and weeds grow side by side
The stronger outdoes the other in stride,
That's how we fare, she gives the lead,
Somewhat dysfunctional, yet I proceed.

Tinkling echoes provoke my heart
When in whisper she tries to impart
Lessons for achieving spiritual growth
And before the Lord enhance my worth.

14. A Dead Heap

A mountain of wasted bodies,
Some mangled, some dismembered,
Remnants of enemies and buddies,
Are ravages the war rendered!

A sight most vile and unnerving,
The outcome of hatred and greed,
A deed so crippling and hurting
Beyond humanity's creed.

War is an inhuman retort
Against all notions of peace
Growth and progress will halt
Without all efforts for truce.

15. We Could Be Their Residue

The pride and arrogance of the Pharisees
And the snobbish hypocrisy of the Scribes,
Filtered down as a dreadful disease
Affected humanity's normal vibes.

The sheer brutality of the Romans,
The unforgettable crimes of Tartars
Unmatched for their violence,
Had paved the way for martyrs.

They feigned to be clever and right
Before the public, the unlettered,
Didn't realize their lack of insight,
But believed they'd been delegated.

Modern men seem their sediments
Filtered through time's liberal sieve,
Camouflaging the dregs as ornaments
Displayed flagrantly out to deceive.

The root of our origin contained the stuff
That sustained our ancestral brigade,
It turned our conscience blunt and rough,
We aren't the people heaven had made.

Horrendous atrocities we blatantly commit
On people and nations far and near,
Reminding a past we refuse to admit
To keep our reputation clean and clear.

We too have our bloodthirsty moods
For gruesome murders and brutal retorts,
We scheme and contrive debased pursuits
And revel in harboring depraved thoughts.

We don't seem to find any difference
For our dealings are quite the same,
We need a rebirth from pristine essence
To support a superior status claim.

16. We're in an Evil Era

An era of evil, bizarre and tangled
In confusing coils we're entangled,
In days of darkness we seek your presence,
We cannot survive in your absence.

Holiness wasn't easy to attain,
And firmly tried their status maintain,
To keep the innocence of body and soul
And obtain heaven, their ultimate goal.

We aren't the people you had fashioned,
The blade of our conscience is rough and blunt,
The path we trudge is rugged and uneven,
With unfocused vision and stained ambition.

This isn't the world you had created
Your initial plan has been awfully distorted,
Its pristine beauty we've surely deformed,
To suit our purpose its features are malformed.

Your bride, the church, now less authentic,
A number of faithful have become skeptic,
Your doctrines seem altered and rolled up in coils,
Some of your ministers are diehard pedophiles.

We are no more your favored images,
Our sins have brought about untold damages,
Your fear of apostasy seems to come true,
For man intents only perdition pursue

Come, Lord and Savior, over us reign,
Our tracks are barred, our efforts in vain,
They say we're in our ultimate days,
Come and rescue us by granting your grace.

17. Words are Treasures

Words are precious gems of the mind
Embodying emotions of every kind,
Written in books and heard in sound
We can't miss them, they're all around.

Visible in tenderness, love and concern,
In kindness, courage and wish to discern,
Floating words on refreshing breeze,
And fragrant words from flowers and trees.

Words in songs of joy and tears,
In shouts and screams of despair and fears,
Written, painted, danced and sung
Are smooth in thought and gentle on tongue.

Words of courage, faith and hope,
To spread knowledge have much scope,
But words of distrust, pride and deceit
Of whose traits are spoken the least.

18. A Visit to Ajna's School

My heart pounded with intense excitement
As I neared the school she had cherished,
That had brought her mental refinement
And a heart with divine love embellished.

My privilege it was to view what she saw,
To walk the paths she frequently trod,
To pray in places she'd wandered in awe,
And linger where she had laughed or sobbed.

Religious sisters and civil teachers
Soaked me in undue praises and honor,
Overwhelmed was I with their gestures
For what I seem to have done for her.

Gripping the trophy close to my heart
With the photos taken for remembrance
Given to me for playing my part
I bid them farewell with due deference.

19. We Hold the Power

We cannot prevent birds
From flying above our heads,
But we can take all care
They build no nests in our hair.

A nest provides protection,
Keeps their eggs in possession,
Till wings and feathers appear
And nestlings bring up the rear.

It'll be a permanent abode
That'll our status corrode,
A nuisance in time to come
To which we could succumb.

Nip in the bud, they say,
It's helpful that we obey,
Regrets could later play
Causing us unending dismay.

20. Suffering and Salvation

Suffering is a path to salvation,
That's what we've been told
By saints in their revelation,
So the same we must uphold.

Walk through the gate of mercy
Enter the home of grace,
In the grand scheme of legacy
Our resilience gets space.

A fertile ground for encounters
Of the mundane kind,
And spiritual refuge in centers
That can foster the mind.

We're perfected through suffering
One that can be redeemed
In the crucible place our offering
To have our fall reversed.

                                            Joe Anthony

C. Life Experiences

Experiences in life shape our beliefs, values, and understanding of the world. We would love to maximize our positive experiences and avoid the negative ones. It is often during these negative, stressful, and challenging times that we find out where our strengths lie, how to push further than we have ever pushed before, and how to truly thrive.

1. Old Age is Beautiful

Only the aged people would know
It is the beauty of this stage,
Many are not so fortunate though
To live to a ripe old age.

Do not consider age in years
It is just a number to arrive,
A state of the mind to let cheers
Keep your failing spirit alive.

Worry not when such feelings unfold
Worry about hating its view,
Never regret about growing up old
It's a privilege granted to a few.

Wrinkled brow and toothless gum
Protruding bones and sunken cheeks,
Bloated belly, turning dumb
Are all God's artistic feats.

Pounds increase and vision blurry,
Aches screaming at every turn,
Crown of grey hair is your glory,
As a reward you must discern.

Old age isn't a way of protest
It's a part of God's specific plan,
It's the season for a harvest
Of the grace you reaped in this span.

After a life of arduous labor
People must retire and rest
Live with dignity and with favor
And a heart bursting with zest.

Aging should not sound so tragic
Instead change the way you age,
You are not old, you are classic,
So live your age, do not change.

                                          Joe Anthony

2. Today My Heart Died

Today the heart in me died
As I knelt before her grave,
Bitterly my spirit cried
For she was young and brave.

Cancer invaded her bones
Sarcoma they had named,
Spread to different zones,
Left her body maimed.

Less than ten was she,
Fought against the plight,
Faith in heaven's decree
Held her spirit upright.

I watched her smile fade
Tears blurred her vision
I kissed her as I prayed
Hoping it came to fruition.

She heard the final alarms
Went with the sinking sun
Into His outstretched arms,
The little innocent one.

At her grave in pain
Unable to restrain the tears
I felt her presence again
That dispelled all my fears.

My heart that had died
Is alive within her soul
She's my angelic guide
To assist me reach my goal.

3. Make Space Within

When your heart is cluttered
Or things within are scattered
No room is enough to contain
The wealth you wish to obtain.

Only the prayer of the humble,
The meek, the mild and the gentle,
And heart that's pure and receptive,
The desired response will receive.

Your faith can't be held hostage,
Nor love detained in bondage,
Unless you submit willingly
Accepting the reality knowingly.

When your energy is involved
To have disputes resolved
You'd have found the space
To live in heaven's embrace.

4. Pilgrims of Hope

Filled with hope and purpose
The pilgrims trudged on
Until next dawn,
Despite the track's surface.

They climbed on leaden feet
Seeking truth,
Meaning of death,
And expiate their life of deceit.

They prayed and sang with fervor
Loud or soft,
Didn't count the cost,
In ardent faith to obtain favor.

They pondered over His essence
Within all beings,
His new teachings
Replete with profound lessons.

Beneath the pulpit of the cross
They celebrated,
Gratitude resonated,
Were ignited to fight for His cause.

5. Blind Performance

A flaring flame carved out a vacuum
After the explosion in the dressing room,
Cinders and ashes spat at me in hate
Couldn't be on stage in such a state.

Time took her steps in measured motion
Helping me reclaim the face I'd chosen,
Hoping to fill the gap without annoyance
But the calm was uneasy in the audience.

The pulse of feelings rose to a state
And the air was thick with voices irate,
When on a sudden the curtain parted,
It was like a smile when anger abated.

The performance evoked wild excitement,
My speech and actions were in alignment
Despite my pain and the loss of sight,
The show was received with utter delight.

After the show they lowered their faces
And heaped upon me lavish praises,
I did the stuff that none ever dared,
Losing my vision when the fire flared.

6. Change in Strategy

She felt no urge to repair the damage
Nor force strong to enthrone courage,
In the throes of guilt and devastation
Felt drowned in the sea of desolation.

Under the shade of a drooping willow,
Where the stunted cactus shrubs grow,
She buries all her past and even dreams
To select the latest and untested schemes.

Many a mile in pursuit she walked,
Met with well-versed agents and talked
To guide and maneuver her next project
And assist her obtain the desired object.

To start the new venture with milieu right,
Her passion and morale now at its height,
She plunged headlong with a mighty force
To employ every available resource.

Lilting and dancing success appeared,
Fragrance of rebirth diffused and cheered,
Bringing her back to a life of content,
A ladder to prop her to higher ascent.

7. Firm Foundation

I have erected a palatial mansion
Love and faith make its foundation,
It will withstand enemy invasion,
Protect its inmates with ardent passion.

With talent and skill I deftly designed,
Manner and course of the work defined,
To each a specific work was assigned
Till every work in its place was aligned.

This building looms now in all its splendor
Portraying a façade of esthetic grandeur,
A major landmark with no contender
Protected by a team to defend her.

8. Peace Displaced Turmoil

Lost in the desert of fatigue and waste
I plodded the wrinkled brow of fate,
That created in time an unsavory taste
Within the receptacle of my estate.

Wilting and waning unable to balance
I struggled to confront the cloud of fear,
I thought my life would sink in silence
For drops of sweat began to appear.

Sloth intruded to drain the fervor,
Strength and vitality before him failed,
Inertia remained a mere observer,
Wasted and spent, my goal was derailed.

I prayed with hope, wanted to be heard,
For I was enthralled by the fragrance of prayer,
Now it was strong enough for heaven to be stirred
So lingered anxiously, awaiting an answer.

No reply came for there was no reaction,
I can't lose hope, for He's benevolent,
There can't be rejection, I was quite certain,
He wouldn't do it, for that was evident.

In the deep silence a door flung open,
An inner experience ardently throbbed,
I received the answer, no word spoken,
A blessed life of peace on me was bestowed.

9. My Cup is Full

My cup's full to the brim
Ready to spill over,
With vigor, vitality and vim
Helps me to stay sober.

Joy, content and peace
Are portions of my core,
That I handle with ease
For my health to restore.

A life agile and active,
Despite its disabilities
That holds me often captive,
Keeps firm, my faculties.

In varied lands I saunter
On highways and bye lanes,
Seeing signs of wonder
In diverse unknown terrains.

Now that my cup is drained,
I have relished the drink,
My goals are all attained,
It's time I fade and shrink.

10. I Heard his Still Voice

The wind was a lion roaring in anger
Growling fiercely, a warning of danger,
Scaring everyone wrecking their choice,
Yet in that chaos I heard His still voice.

Thunder erupted mercilessly loud
Cracking to pieces every roaming cloud
Piercing the eardrums by its sharp noise
Yet in that confusion I heard His still voice.

The earth exploded in violent temper
Rattled every object from its center,
Splitting apart the monolithic terrain,
Yet in that havoc His still voice did reign.

Tsunami raged with revengeful fury
Disfiguring the earth and the open sea,
The thunder of water on the shore was heard
Yet in that mayhem His still voice stirred.

When lightning struck, harsh was the blaze
Roaring like wild boars wounded in chase,
As the angry flames ravaged all nature
I heard his still voice smile in rapture.

Despite such bizarre events in creation
Friendship and concern can maintain relation,
They provide reasons for us to rejoice
And hear distinctly that ever still voice.

11. A Tragic Birthday

The joy of a birthday was diffused all over,
But its fragrance was mild and sober,
Sitting solemnly a cake with a candle
Was conspicuous upon a decked up table.

The temper and mood of this formal function
Demanded an exclusive celebration,
It is the farewell to her teenage years
Before she stepped into new frontiers.

Only the best of her friends were invited,
Certainly they were greatly delighted,
She was a person of beauty and repute
Admired for her judgments astute.

The phone screamed in an unusual fashion,
Echoed loudly all about the mansion,
A mournful whisper announced the arrival
Of her body that struggled for survival.

Abruptly occurred this severe accident,
They couldn't save her for death was instant,
Doctors declared that she was brought dead
Due to the injury suffered on her head.

A tragedy ended this beautiful life
And every heart with sorrow was rife,
Desolate and broken everyone wept,
The pain was extreme and difficult to accept.

12. A Glass Bottle

Be careful how you handle me
For I am made of glass
I can contain all you wish
And transparently too.

If you hold me by my neck
Keep a hand at the bottom
My neck can crack with pressure
And cut your fingers to bleed.

If by chance you drop me
I'll be in many pieces
Gather them gently with care
Lest they slice your hand.

13. Plain Truth

We breathe the air of truth unvarnished
Plain and simple to fathom,
Our breath entails a conscience untarnished
Leading to a unity at random.

Healing rays that profusely emanate
From such a sincere source,
Create a steadfast ripple effect
Redesigning our life's course.

What can make or mar our vision
As we employ our resources
It's the caliber for prudent decision
Despite opposing forces.

14. My Life is an Edifice

My life is an edifice, complex and mysterious
Flesh and bones are the cement and bricks,
Knitted together by wires of nerves,
Given energy by the breath of His nostrils.

Veins and tissues merging in unison
Engage every part in tender fusion,
Soft and firm organs meet to conform
Tasks that need assistance to perform.

Centralized system of communication
Controlled by the brain in coordination
With other agents potent and vital
Makes this building a magnificent mortal.

15. The Circle Effect

Benumbed senses weary of motion
Floated aimlessly in a sleepy ocean,
Devoid of stamina or the urge to revive
Drifted in abeyance afraid to survive.

Enclosed in a circle without any exits
Confines of a prisoner it truly depicts,
They kiss the edge of the endless curve
Hating limits to freedom they deserve.

Despair and anguish prolong the ache
Waking all senses to reason partake,
Only firm resolve can lift the barrier
Bring in freedom to restart a career.

16. A World in Turmoil

The looming specter of a world in turmoil
And nations in conflicts ever on the boil,
A world teetering on the brink of chaos,
People left grappling with uncertain loss,
A church splintered to varied directions
Challenging the very basic foundations,
An uncertain future of faith and existence
Rippling across the world in dissonance:

These are highly disturbing disasters
Our resolute attention certainly matters.
Come before Him in humble demeanor,
Offer your prayers profound and sincere,
His remedy is effective, you can't surmise
In His dealings he doesn't compromise.

17. Swimming in a Cesspool

He was a capable leader
Firm and resolute,
Adulation raised him a wielder,
A mighty despot.

Crime of corruption, his game,
A player astute,
Pride and greed spat shame
In brutal refute.

Down the cesspool of guilt
Of opium haze,
His mind blistered in conflict
In deep malaise.

Soon the smell of sin
Emerged and spread,
Nauseating him within
Reeling his head.

Laid on the palm of sorrow
With shame dripping,
Thought of the past and morrow
His conscience pricking.

Drenched in blood and sweat
Repentance emerged,
Discarded every form of threat
His hope surged.

18. A Treasure Trove

Scanning the attic in a dark night
With a beaming torch in my hand
In the presence of the old man despite
A treasure trove of surprises in demand
Scattered about was an awesome sight.

Roused by a deceptive sense of trust
And besieged by curiosity and despair.
To an uneasy feeling I couldn't adjust
Clung to my skeleton making me aware
That this attraction I must resist.

Navigating through my feelings of shame
Immersing myself in the rhythm of work
Withdrew stealthily from every blame
Leaving behind all the forbidden stock
For the old man to bear the shame.

19. The Final Journey

Sailing along the morning breeze
Passing above tall pine trees,
I heard voices calling me loud
Concealed behind a fleecy cloud.

In voice determined and compelling,
Warned I would soon leave my dwelling,
So get prepared, no longer delay,
Renounce all that is barring my way.

Despite relationships holding me back
I'm determined to pursue this track,
When I turn to bid them farewell
They'd be weeping, I can foretell.

At night I dreamed of a clear morning
Bright and beautiful, highly rewarding,
All pain faded beyond the horizon
I found myself in a cheerful environ.

I felt picked up and borne by an eagle
Even though I wasn't weary or feeble
My heart throbbed in profound ecstasy
As we glided beyond the sea.

Let me sip the nectar of mountains,
Cross barriers and break all chains,
Listen to the song in the valley pervades
Before all beauty and fantasy fades.

The mountains sang, the flowers smiled,
Their beauty and brightness got aligned
Beckoning me to the pearl-set portal
Where I shall enjoy a life immortal.

20. Thought-Provoking

The canvas of my heart displays
A precious painting pleasing to view,
Sentiments of sympathy it conveys,
Evokes joyful emotions too.

An emaciated boy of seven
Holds an infant on his hip,
Shares a lollipop half-eaten,
A prized asset in secure grip.

Sweet and rewarding are the drips
An overflow of its contentment
That escapes from its smiling lips,
Though every drop is important.

Sparkling eyes of pride and delight,
Result of the infant's lingering taste,
Cast a ray of joyous sight
On viewers who can truly relate.

21. A Sincere Promise

I won't condemn you nor will I hate,
Betray you in anyway, nor castigate,
Because you are mine in every sense
For your malice I won't take offence.

You may slander me or may praise,
Distance yourself from my race,
I shall assist you in your quest
And grant willingly your request.

I want to love you in all respects,
Support all your ambitious projects,
Help you to review every venture,
Accept life as an exciting adventure.

22. The Normal

I smiled at a beggar
Gave him a tiny coin,
He saw heaven therein
It tasted just like sugar.

She was an aged woman
Limping on swollen feet,
Gave her beside me a seat
I thought it was human.

My acts I thought trivial
Noting important or great
But easily they could relate
As they viewed them vital.

23. The Way They Work

Clap for the person who trudges in anguish
Making every effort his duty accomplish,
Tough and harsh may his project depict
Needing unexpected maneuvers on sight.

The mediocre worker puts lukewarm effort
Sweating profusely as if digging a desert,
Minimal output, though harder the labor
Should he deserve equal praise and honor?

Flowers could be tiny or large in size
We've no reason to praise or despise,
They all fade away having succeeded
And all their tasks, carefully completed.

24. When Old Age Creeps In

Some age gracefully without strain or stress
Wrinkled though their brow may appear,
Their face is fresh and smile sincere
Evinces no sign of inertia or distress.

Others are full of tension and fear,
Anxiety tearing their heart asunder,
Against their will they submit and surrender,
To live in conditions woeful and austere.

Physically weak and helpless for reasons,
Pain screaming through their spine and neck
Makes their life a miserable wreck
While their longing for sympathy deepens.

Hard of hearing and vision decreasing
Depending on wheelchairs or on crutches,
Despite the attendant's surly grudges
They live always on others depending.

Tongue isn't flexible so words unspoken
Unable to express their wants and desires,
Even to the dearest they seem a nuisance
Demanding they give their constant attention.

Devastated interiorly and feeling guilty
Powerless to come up to their expectations,
Adequately meet their own obligations
Forever considered a major casualty.

To perform as they did in younger days,
Unable to keep up even with the smallest,
Left behind by the slowest and the weakest
And bring up the rear despite the delays.

Emotions hurl their spirit into desolation
Torture their mind and wrench their heart,
Helplessly aware they can't play their part
Sink into the sea of dejection and isolation.

Tears keep dripping from the edge of their eyelids
Their heart torn apart from extreme helplessness
Their shriveled frame wrapped in all its tightness
Consumes their will power and resistance forbids.

They see themselves dwindle and fade
Falling below the terrain of clod,
Six feet below is their temporary ward
To leave for their home the Lord had made.

25. An Evil Queen

Between layers of legends and myths
Her life was concealed,
It wasn't unraveled
For fear of instant and traumatic deaths.

In the tapestry of her mysterious tale
Her legacy displayed,
Its worth downplayed,
For truth they followed a murky trail.

Her memory pervaded the ambiance,
Her life and legacy
And her disloyalty,
Overshadowed her significance.

Fueled by commitment the searchers pursued
With unwavering faith,
To confront the wraith,
But none of them returned to confirm the truth.

26. Faulty Approach

We linger on objects most trivial
Focusing more on the external,
Leap and skip over matters crucial,
Ignore the very core, that's eternal.

We're in awe of blissful scenes
Imbibe them eagerly without pause,
Bypass the crown to gather pennies
Elated to receive a transient applause.

We acclaim people's amazing feats
Emulate some with hidden pleasure,
Oblivious of all blatant mistreats
We heap on servants at our leisure.

A deep insight into figures and facts
In-depth knowledge of all essentials
Prowess to dissect and examine acts
Will confirm and validate our credentials.

27. Overambitious

When we move on two feet
We think we own the street,
When the sky seems reachable
Our soaring plans look viable.

If our feet take a tumble
And our ambitions futile,
We'll learn to be humble
And plough a field fertile.

If we're involved in ventures
Focusing only on success,
The result of our adventures
Needn't claim to bring progress.

The chaff then be our element
Blown about by the gust,
Being no more relevant
A worthless scoop of dust.

28. A Master Smuggler

Satan smuggles into your mind
Things untrue and vile,
Penetrates through ways unkind,
Relegates to the void our profile.

His aims and dealings are covert,
Stalks on tip-toe and sneaks,
A shameless and devious pervert,
His entire body reeks.

Murky and dubious, his envoys,
His hideous canons impart,
Ways and means he deploys
To convert a consenting heart.

He cannot accept defeats
Raves in violent anger,
A veritable hell he creates
Engulfed in deadly rancor.

He exploits our doubts and weakness
Inflates to boost its volume,
To convince us of the bleakness
Of heaven's strength we assume.

Fear not his sordid designs
Nor his enticing allure,
Because in love He enshrines
And keeps us from harm secure.

29. The Spider Web

The spider on the web hugging the wall
Has been trying to jump and crawl,
He moves in ominous and uncanny fashion
In surprising speed with extreme passion.

The owner guarding this strategic castle
Is seldom seen waging any real battle,
He's just a dot on the wild web's world
Often he is spotted crouched and curled.

More than once he's faced the broom,
Like a guilty child then left the room,
Undaunted the figure returned later
Posing himself as a casual visitor.

His presence was a sheer distraction
An alarming cause for stringent action,
A bunch of creepy feet explored my face
Leaving me in disgust and in disgrace.

My maid took a bolder decision
Resolved to follow a course of collision,
Sprayed a lethal liquid on every wall
That left no trace of the spider in the hall.

I can recall him dive to the depth
Like a rider measure the well of death,
Rise again with an elastic spring
And dangle from a slender string.

Never a spider dared to encroach
Or ventured near the margin approach,
The memory of that tragic event
Is even now an effective deterrent.

30. The Genocide

Caesar ordered the genocide
Of males under two
Rivals stepped aside
To help his scheme pursue.

No challenge is accepted
Against his authority
Dare anyone defected
Would end in obscurity.

Violence in every city
Blood in every street
No one pleaded guilty
Though murders complete.

The Holy Family left
Made a quick exit
Over Judean desert
Into pharaoh's Egypt.

An unwed woman
Clothed in poverty
Sought to trudge a nation
Entangled in sorcery

Seven years in exile
They had made amends
Away all the while
From family and friends.

Gratefully they retraced
The path they once trod
Relieved of being graced
With their loving God.

31. The Disowned

Plodding the desert bleakness
Where expectations dwindled,
Lost in the dismal barrenness
All calculations tumbled,
In the harsh hour in weakness
The feeble man stumbled,
Fleeing the evil of darkness
His wicked sons had created.

Forlorn he was sheltered
In the shade of an oak tree,
In the hot summer sweltered
As he lay helpless and weary,
Feeling his spirit altered,
Utterly drained of energy
His sons' ingratitude recalled
He felt his eyes grow bleary.

Dejected and dismayed he laid
His weary head on his palm,
Against a tree trunk as bed
Undisturbed in blissful calm,
The eternal sleep of the dead
Caressed him with soothing balm.
The sons on the scene landed
But didn't show any qualms.

They felt defeated and crushed,
Their ambition was thwarted
For too late they appeared
To attend to the final need
Of the man who refused to cede
His estate they hadn't deserved,
All his life he was disowned
A severe disaster, they reckoned.

32. Tranquilly we Lived

Tranquil was the life we lived,
Its corridors simplicity echoed,
The rhythm of the past didn't blend
With the new unusual trend.

Prayers echoed through aisles
In varied voices and styles
Retelling tales of the past
Hoping they would outlast.

Mystical and spiritual entwined
And earth and heavens designed
To bridge the gap between man's
And God's divine plans.

An unsettling sense of unease
Seemed to emerge and increase
Echoing from an unknown
And a mysterious zone.

Trumpets blared through the wall
Was heaven's wakeup call
Predicting a cosmic upheaval
To help our hope's retrieval.

33. An Evil Generation

This era is full of mysterious tangles
Trapping the gullible from all angles,
Enticing them with appealing pleasure
Compelling with a magnetic pressure.

Demonic agents are ever on the prowl
Concealing danger in actions most foul,
Wickedness steeped in the wine of malice
Is offered as authentic in a sacred chalice.

This era throttles all attempts to change,
Brings about clarity so truth looks strange,
Defaced by smearing the fine soot of vice
Agrees in general as a valid device.

Let all humanity its burden unload
Into the comforting arms of the Lord,
There isn't alternate agent or route
To assist you in your relentless pursuit.

34. For a Good Harvest

The world's our field to sow
All that we need to grow,
With sweat and labor mow
The harsh ridge and furrow.

Our struggle will yield a bounty
Though rain supply be scanty,
The harvest will bring in plenty
And keep filling our pantry.

Our blood will nourish the soil
With our unceasing toil,
The enemy will certainly recoil
From trying our endeavor spoil.

35. Revisiting Ajna

My soul flew on the wings of an arrow
Penetrating walls of light and shadow,
Eager to kneel at a favorite sight
And in deep reverence prayers recite.

Here her body was laid to rest,
She was only a short-term guest,
This soil has claimed her body revered
As a person to all she endeared.

To salute this leader par excellence
And admire her deep benevolence,
To thank her for being the inspiration
And a catalyst for my transformation.

A year has passed since my last visit,
Such long duration I couldn't resist,
Nothing has changed externally though
Her spirit impacted me, I surely know.

36. The Corrupt Lawyer

Justice entered the lawyer's booth
Holding up a statue blindfolded,
With mass scale sideways tilted
Accusing him as an unfair sleuth.

A client's beauty can alter the truth
Ignoring the spirit of the law,
Distort facts to create flaws
And highlight them for an untruth.

Justice pronounced a severe verdict
Against the attorney's unfair deals,
Deprived him the right to make appeals,
Delivered him to the court as a convict.

37. Man's Concept of Law

Law is a name that is held in abhorrence
Until its undisclosed sense is revealed,
Then it gains global significance,
And becomes everyone's favored password.

Mercy drops falling on soil without hope
Stirring forth life of the spirit divine
Urging and helping the soul to elope
Hand in hand towards a sphere benign.

Like the morning rays caressing a bloom
To warm and nurse it to face the onslaught,
Like a shower on the earth nearing its doom
Infusing an existence that was long sought.

When struggle is most severe happiness glows,
A wounded beast is able to better defend,
The heat on the cake its true nature bestows,
Such is the direction that all our Laws trend.

                                                  Joe Anthony

D. In Nature's Bosom

Nature, majestic in all its beauty, grandeur, glamor and spell, reflects its Creator who is the Supreme Beauty. To observe and penetrate the depth of nature is a divine talent freely bestowed on man. It is not the perquisite of everyone to enter that pure ecstatic domain to savor the delicacy laid out for the eye and the heart. People with a receptive heart, purity of mind, and simplicity of spirit can appreciate and relish beauty in its myriad forms.

1. Spring Time

Spring plays games with leaves,
Tickles their new born nerves,
Paints their face light green,
Keeps them cool and serene.

Colors explode in gardens
When spring her eyes opens,
Flowers dance gaily on twigs
As the breeze kisses their lips.

Bees and butterflies flutter,
In jubilant sentiments cluster,
Draining the concealed nectar
Held in the receptacle's shelter.

Bathed in the fragrance of nature
The ambiance is alive to nurture
Creation's varied existence,
And maintain its exuberance.

2. Beautiful Desert

Amidst the expanse of an arid terrain
They live in conflict and strife,
A mesmerizing blend of joy and pain
Shapes the rhythm of their life.

Against the ruthless truth of the desert
The Bedouin resilience is amazing
A surreal fusion of dew and drought
In desperate need of refreshing.

The undulating sands heave to compete
Beauty and wonder retain,
But life moves on camel feet
With only a whisper of rain.

Caught in a whirlwind the sands collide
With rocks and caravans alike,
The golden sand dunes seem to slide
As if taking a hike.

The soulful beauty of solitude and silence
Is a magic hard to define,
Vibrant desert blooms on cactus' essence
Make an onlooker benign.

3. Beneath the Frozen Turf

Beneath the snow mantle white and pure
Stashed away among the roots of a grove
A seed lay dormant but aware and sure
Awaiting spring time to wake up and rove.

Sunbeams pierce the outer surface
Injecting energy to rise up and grow,
Beneath the cold turf in limited place
Inhaling the warmth diffused below.

Limbs and organs strain to emerge
In uniform effort to assert zest,
In time it took sufficient courage
To encounter a world offering the best.

Slow and steady it sprouted and grew
Secure and cozy in a unique setting,
Ready to blend with an ambience new
And enjoy a life so fruitful and fitting.

4. A Romantic Scene

The sun peered out early one morning
Saw the placid ocean fresh and enticing,
Tenderly cushioned her in an embrace
And planted a kiss on her smiling face.

The stars were winking and wooing the moon
Timid and shy, though it was still noon,
The sky dropped down a cloud for a screen
To conceal what's going on behind the scene.

Softly the breeze whispered endearing words
To trees enamored by the song of birds,
Butterflies on flowers were seen to parade
With bees humming an idyllic serenade.

A cloud enwrapped all in a fond cuddle
Heartwarming was their prolonged snuggle
Eloped with everyone to a celestial abode
Eternal happiness had on them bestowed.

5. A Ripe Old Leaf

A ripe old leaf whose course has run,
My purpose in life has just been done,
I don't produce life's sap anymore,
Nor any food for the stem I store.

The branch of my birth has rejected me,
New leaves refresh the look of the tree,
I'm pushed down to the very last brink,
Detached from life I fall and sink.

The wind mournfully sighs and blows,
Gently and silently I drift to the lows,
Fall and rest with dry leaves galore
Scattered about on the arid floor.

We're raked and piled into little peaks,
Burnt or dumped underground for weeks,
To become food for a new generation
Of trees in the process of fresh creation.

6. A Blissful Atmosphere

On the lips of a rosebud the sunbeams kissed
And transformed it into a blossom exquisite,
The caress of the breeze was gentle and warm
It penetrated deep with energy and charm.

The bees serenaded with gauzy wings,
Butterflies flaunted their colored awnings,
The flower beamed brightly diffusing scent,
Awakening a thrill that had been dormant.

The glow of the rainbow that fringed the sky
Decked her in a mantle pleasing to the eye,
The mist of gloom that hovered above
Was replaced by energy derived from love.

Inhaling the aromas of rebirth and freshness
And wrapped in the colors and sounds of goodness
This flower stepped into a brand new season
Bouncing herself free in wild abandon.

7. Diffuse the Fragrance

Diffuse the fragrance of compassion,
With radiant smiles of patience,
Adorn their cloudy ambience
And color that bleak horizon.

Unfurl the vows of devotion,
Wipe away the mist of doubt,
Let the seed of love sprout,
A shade for your protection.

Let success breathe out delight
And dance in the astral domain
Attuned to a romantic strain
In a poetic message ignite.

Passion embraces desires
Impacts the pitch of their urge,
Often it brings out a purge,
Then such passion inspires.

8. In the Arms of Night and Day

Night is a perfume that envelops me,
Smoothly I float on its invisible waves,
Though I'm hidden in a darkened alley
Angels pry out to watch my moves.

Morning hugs me with refreshing aroma
Rousing me to follow a life of action,
Daylight gives me an enthused persona
Filling me with gratitude and devotion.

Nights and days are twins of a kind
They have nothing in common between,
Yet they possess a unique mind
Which is protected and can't be seen.

9. Her Lonely Home

Deep in a virgin greenwood mead
Alone she roamed at leisurely speed,
Glad to get out of her cottage rare
And inhale the mist soaked morning air.

A recluse by nature she lives alone,
Feverish life-style she wishes to disown,
An environ of silence soft and serene
And the echo of a birdsong in between.

She pens poems of angelic nature
Inspired by the spirit in rapture,
Sets them to music and sings all night
Enthralls the ambience with extreme delight.

Friends or visitors do not frequent
This idyllic dwelling concealed by intent,
Her life is full, to the fullest she lives
Content with all the joy she derives.

10. The Mountain River

A narrow river winding down slopes
Is beguiling for the eyes to behold,
The enchanting sights before us unfold
Is a scenic view of curves and loops.

The river is a pack of energy and force
When it strikes a hurdle awry,
Here the water sprays up the sky
Holding a rainbow's beauty perforce.

The river swells in volume and size,
Enters the plane in separate ways,
Ever on the move, forward always,
To fill the ocean with refreshing supplies.

Every obstacle we must subdue,
Like the river, follow set course,
Gently and smoothly or even by force
That bar our efforts to seek and pursue.

11. The Sea and The Sky

The sea is a vast and endless field
Alive with life of every kind,
A mural of exquisite beauty held
To mesmerize even the deaf and the blind,

Filled with varied paintings and sketches
Vibrant with colors your eyes can't defy,
A tapestry of pleasing sights that stretches
Beneath an immense and stately sky.

The sky reflects the endless sea,
Displays celestial objects and beings
That with the creatures of the sea agree
To reveal the actual faces of things.

The sky and the sea are the two faces
The Almighty has fashioned at His will,
Where one begins the other ceases
None knows nor can they figure out still.

12. To The End of the Earth

I want to travel to the ends of the earth
To meet people of an assorted kind,
Spend time with them in the land of their birth
For proof authentic and defined.

People with outlook completely different
Strange, whimsical, silly or pervert,
Who believe in dubious gods virulent
And obstinately all changes reject.

I want to know their habits and customs
For I know some are odd and outrageous
I need to see to believe their systems
And be aware if they're truly tenacious.

Their food is said to be insipid and bland
They cook, or burn, or eat just raw,
Whether meat or vegetable, both in demand,
And permitted by their country's law.

Their outfits reflect their land's profile
Off-white or colored, loose or long,
Some go unclothed like the soil sterile,
But beard and headgear must go along.

It's a wonder how they came to exist,
Did humans or some mightier decide,
To conjure up this mysterious and secret tryst
And take the gullible for a pleasure ride!

13. The Tyrant Sun

The sun provides us with life and vigor
When he can control his unwieldy temper,
Let heaven help us when he gets furious
The extent of damage can surely be serious.

The sun was a tyrant wielding a sword
Of flame that burnt and wildly roared,
Sitting on his blazing throne in the sky
His malicious intent we failed to espy.

Scorching the earth and all it contains,
Pounding relentlessly, lacking restraints,
Deforming features unique in grade,
Causing the status of life to degrade.

Roasting the soil to prevent any growth
Of food essential for life on the earth,
Killing all fauna to prevent their escape
And leaving a glaring arid landscape.

14. The Wintry Wind

The wintry wind with sharp steel edge
Slashed the air with all its steam,
Speeding in fury to outdo the sunbeam
Gradually it climbed the mountain ridge.

It flowed in directions without any warning
Deflecting swiftly like an aimless bird,
Twisting and turning in speed undeterred
Bringing disaster, abrupt and alarming.

It's mild and smooth when the sun sinks low
Framing an ambiance of elegance serene,
Rippling waves flaunting a glossy sheen
As the wind sails on the water below.

Random in direction, speed and force
It could unsettle the flow of thought,
Alter the motion your mind had sought
To wage a battle or peace enforce.

15. Rest Before the Quest

From flower to flower I nimbly flitter
In the breezy morning's crystalline glitter,
Plunging into the core of a daisy
To relish its fragrant flavor in ecstasy.

Delicious indeed is the nectar I imbibe,
Its odor creates a sublime vibe,
Tipsy in every sense and emotion
I'm a lethargic mass in fusion.

Now I'm cruising in a mystical sea
Floating evenly on a slumbering spree,
Wake me not from my well-earned rest
Before I begin my forthcoming quest.

16. The Brighter Side

From dust to solids,
From smile to words,
From winter to spring
From night to morning,
Let your light shine

From clutter to space,
From sin to grace,
From hatred to love,
From death to life,
Let your faith inspire.

From buds to flowers,
From drought to showers,
From detach to align,
From human to divine,
Let your hope mature.

From husk on the seed,
From frost on the thorn,
From knife at the wound,
From the womb to the tomb,
Let your life be complete.

17. Beauty Revealed the Truth

Peeping through the morning mist
Sweeping over the open field
She strained her eyes unable to resist
Nature's beauty the fog concealed.

Delightful feelings of healthy freshness,
Awesome colors that charm the eye,
Breezes stirring the leaves in stillness,
Arouse emotions that welcome or defy.

Mountain calmness made her nostalgic,
Blurred visions of childhood appeared,
Many were pleasing, some though tragic,
Most she relished but others she feared.

Adorning lies and falsehood with beauty
Her life was depicted with deceitful images,
Now this new scene pleasing and pretty
Offered her many unsought privileges.

18. Healthy Morning Air

Awesome is the view and so is the feeling
When you sit in your balcony in the morning,
Fresh and clean is the breezes that hug you
Sweeping across the sea, your spirit renew.

Pure and soft is its flowing motion
Inhale without any effort or notion,
Fill your lungs with the abundance of nature
Enjoy the satisfaction offered as a favor.

Noon onwards the air becomes heavy
Breathing does not come as that easy,
Start the day with lungs full of freshness,
Reach the day's end buttressed by its stillness.

19. The Garden Within

There's a garden within every man
Enter this inner world and explore,
The beauty you often fail to scan
Is lavishly spread, do not ignore.

Delve into the core of this space,
Journey to the endless expanse,
Seek out the beauty of His grace
That will send you into a trance.

Come with me to my inner world
A world of wonder filled with marvels,
Search for the author who has unfurled
And proclaimed it through his Gospels.

Joe Anthony

E. Penetrate the Enigma

An enigma is something difficult to understand or explain, inscrutable or mysterious. An enigmatic person is a mystery, a problem, a puzzle, or a riddle. You never know what really that person is thinking, or what his or her motives for doing certain things are. Enigma applies to utterance or behavior that is very difficult to interpret.

1. She was Different

I remember her as a pensive child
Sitting at the window all beguiled,
Watching the sparrows and other birds,
Talking to them in gestures and words.

Flowers and trees in the nearby garden
Constructed for her a spiritual den,
Endless was the time she spend viewing
And a formlessness she kept wooing.

Her mind was unusual, an utter marvel,
Enigmatic events she could unravel,
Predict the nature of uncanny events,
Verify the validity of their contents.

She kept aloof and chose to acquire
Knowledge and values that could inspire,
The public decided to consider her weird,
For her intimates deemed her revered.

2. A Mystical Experience

On sun-drenched noonday trail
Of swaying water's verge,
I float at ease and sail
Hearing a melody emerge
Resonating from the deep.

In unison I join the strain,
A lilting dulcet song
That can soothe and sustain
And ripples of joy prolong,
Energizing the water's surface.

Life swimming below me
Braid along my dreams
Fusing as one in the sea,
And my reflection beams,
Forging a lasting union.

Caressed by the rays of the sun,
Hugged by the warmth of water,
Music in motion and fun,
This treat of love and laughter
Was a mystical experience.

3. An Ancient Manuscript

Tucked hidden between faded pages
Of an old book gone through ravages
By time and usage having laid waste,
It isn't worth while searching in haste.

Precious may be the matter recovered
From this book that fractures suffered,
For crisp and brittle in form it appeared
With a layer of dust all over smeared.

Delicate fingertips scanned its surface
Probing the nature of is resilience,
An extra pressure could cause much damage
And all the wealth would end up as garbage.

Patience and careful procedure resulted
Success for which everyone exulted,
Gems of wisdom concealed by a prophet
For humanity's benefit or for its regret.

4. Destiny

We are machines in the hand of fate
Grinding at the giant wheel desolate,
Wearing out energy in endless wait
For destiny's terms our life to dictate.

Succumbing to a predetermined force
Needn't be the priority of our course,
The relevant side lane offered at source
Must be the only one we should endorse.

Destiny can't make or mar our future
There's a power far beyond its nature,
Suffice to trust and submit as a creature
To God's gracious and divine feature.

5. Invest in Fullness

Emptiness is a vacuum
Lonely like a tomb,
Discard, it's futile,
Makes you servile.

Submerged in despair
In pursuit beware,
Skeleton feigns shape,
Prevents your escape.

When chasm looms
Emits toxic fumes,
Waste not labor
For a trifling cipher.

With conscience clean
And your vision keen
View things with caution,
For a life of fruition.

6. Natural Bonding

The infant looked at the mother's face
Thought her smile meant a kiss,
Stirred avidly and rolled to her place
To enjoy that cherished bliss.

The mother was enjoying a pleasant dream
It traced a smile on her lips,
The baby's breath on her face was a scream,
A reaction of a rare mix.

Instantly she rolled over to the child
Hugged her close to her breast,
Her eyes spoke in a language mild
A delightful shock at its best.

A mother's empathy with her infant,
All physical distance despite,
Reflects that bonding, in an instant,
Of a creature, the creator's invite.

7. Crossing the Hurdle

Like a young tree despoiled of leaves
Ugly and repelling to a keen observer,
Or sheep that's shorn off its fleece
When in strain their bodies maneuver,
He's been moving by touch than sight
Unable to focus as doubt runs rife.
If God has joined the dots aright
He's to walk the line to avoid strife.

A gnawing fear grips his heart,
A storm of screams rips him apart,
Wrenches him by force out of his trance
And leaves him alone at Truth's entrance.
Not a sliver of hope appears,
Faith has slipped into oblivion,
Resistance does not allay fears,
Distress mars his nurtured mission.

Jonah's complex grips his controls,
He can't confront his face in the mirror
Prefers to evade his destined goals
And beep faintly in time's monitor.
A crucial encounter alters his stance
Urges him to employ unused talents,
Stirs his mindset to further advance
And observe all the former covenants.

The burning torch of faith rekindles,
Its radiance reveals a distinct vision,
Hope grows strong and contrast dwindles,
He moves towards a resolute decision.

Head held high, his stride in control,
Undaunted he weathers every storm,
Proceeds with conviction towards his goal
Alerts his faculties to brace and perform.

8. Time is a Mystery

Time is a mystery
None can deny,
Its laughter and cry
Can agree or defy.

Time gives gladness
In limitless dose,
So too dense sadness
To leave you morose.

It leaps and scales
In avid fashion,
Or lingers like snails
In pesky motion.

It's punctual for some
Though not so often,
Too early to come
Or the late option.

Time is enjoyment
Or can be pain,
Time can't prevent
Our stress or strain.

Time can be night
Projecting fear,
Or a day bright
Serene and clear.

Let time be a friend
For our welfare,
We can depend
Upon his care.

9. Life in a Granite Chunk

This stone is a cold unyielding granite,
Despite the prevailing warmth of the night
Or the blazing heat of the summer noon
Can't diffuse energy even in June.

You may chip or carve trying to transform
That's trapped inside this shapeless form,
Hit or scrape it in rhythmic motion
To exhibit this gloriously unique creation.

You could add texture to refine it a marvel,
Boost its finish with glow and sparkle,
Present a gorgeous beauty in splendor,
Always alive in regal grandeur.

You have fashioned a stunning handiwork
Infused life and zest into a rock,
An awesome wonder to inspire a viewer
Who could even be its proud possessor.

10. Fancy

Fancy is a cloud of melodious strain
Floating aimlessly within your brain,
Foamless it adjusts in every void,
Prefers to stay up and be employed.

Lucid in motion, can vanish at will,
Take up velocity or remain still,
With pomp and splendor emerge in might,
But its conscience is never contrite.

Whimsical by nature impish and mean
Always among the self-assertive are seen,
Rarely found among poets and seers
Who do not search or wish for careers.

11. Like The Grain of Wheat

My mind slipped down a world of pain,
Exceeding sorrow wrapped me insane,
Never imagined my work would be spurned,
By those who had their prestige confirmed.

Assuming I be the seed considered
That will create life only when dead,
So my effort will be eventually rewarded
When in memory my name's recorded.

Take heart my soul, be not afraid
You'll receive in full what you've deserved,
Your delight won't be when you're alive
But surely when in heaven you arrive.

12. Interior Conflict

She stood silently by the window in pain
Watching fat raindrops tap on the pane,
And treetops swaying in manner insane
In fury untamed, unable to restrain.

Alone in torments she ponders her plight
Searching for comfort nowhere in sight,
The bitter cup offered her brings no respite,
Distraught, she decides to retire for the night.

Foreign agents her weary mind explore,
Uncanny images never seen before,
Confused and crushed she seems to implore
That they should avoid hurting her more.

Sleep came on tiptoe to soothe her strained eyes
And anoint her nerves with whispering sighs,
In dream she felt her weightless form rise
Propelled by a mysterious pleasing device.

13. Sterile Outlook

Desperate attempts are the only way
To bridge the gap of apathy and delay,
It's like foam bubbles devoid of pith
Abstract and surreal, an ancient myth.

Things are sterile, arid and bleak,
Trees put on blatantly a bony physique,
Plants bear no flowers despite the feeds,
If flowers ever bloom they bear no seeds.

Devoid of stamina deprived of urge
All elements need an immediate purge,
People and animals soaked in sloth
Fail to provide any effective growth.

A rebirth of courage to invest and prosper,
A desire to live a life more proper,
And effort to achieve a definitive goal,
Can bring these agents under control.

14. Source of Wisdom

Words of wisdom can flow over
From a vile and filthy mouth,
The devil is good at quoting the Scripture
To support his idea of truth.

Whispers heard from a charming person
Can inspire and stir the heart,
Insipid may be that was spoken
And the tongue becomes an ugly dart.

Imagine love in the hearts of men
Who seek only wealth and fame,
Glory and honor promote ambition
Reject religion and God's name.

Wisdom presents truth as real
Only the candid are able to discern,
For common folks it's an ordeal
Such affairs are not their concern.

15. Beware

Peeping through a window in a lonely night
I saw despair and fear creeping,
Moonbeams replacing the candle light
Revealed a vague form cautiously sneaking.

Pregnant with deceit this wanton image
Was the wild hunger searching for the pure,
Crawling about to inflict much damage
On innocents it's keen to meet and allure.

Let us be warned of the intent and purpose
Concealed artfully to beguile the viewer,
Beneath a trap of an appealing surface
Wanting to tempt an amateur consumer.

16. Time is Dying

Time is an unyielding specter
That looms as a ruler's scepter,
Bars us with menacing stance
Refusing for freedom a chance.

The riddle echoing through time
Reveals its vile head of crime,
On the brink of a critical end
Fed with venom by the fiend.

Time's eroded by infection
Of human sins of passion,
By thirst for power driven
Unleashes chaos and ruin.

Ravaged by forces malignant
And agents whose zeal is stagnant,
The fabric of time is woven
To reflect value's erosion.

17. He Enters Undetected

What we dread the most at times
Abruptly creeps in life outright,
Stubbornly clings on like a parasite
Even prepared to perpetrate crimes.

We're required to detach its tentacles
Embedded deeply in our essence,
An agent to eclipse our real presence
We need to stay within our cubicles.

We can't escape their constant onslaught
They track down easily our every move,
Their control on us we can disprove
If we are persistent in our effort.

Only our faith can remedy obtain,
And escort us beyond all borders,
Frees us from inner disorders
Elevates our status to a superior plane.

18. We are his Miracles

Man is the living miracle
Creation's undisputed pinnacle,
Each with features unique
Not one is entirely alike.

His mind is to rule the heart
But often it isn't that,
For emotion takes over charge
And leaves the mind at large.

Reason is enthroned in the mind
And feelings in the heart enshrined,
Each is essential for the person
For the miracle named human.

19. In a Fancy Mood

My fancy buoyantly flapping its wings
Across a precipice in violent swings,
Its exuberance is beyond control
For it is urgent to achieve its goal.

Beguiled and absorbed by an alien scene
With sparkle of colors blending serene,
Breathing its image in vibrant emotion
Offers with panache an ecstatic vision.

Lulled in this ambience my spirit deems
To sail on the rhythmic cadence of dreams,
Float on the waves of surreal fragrance
And inhale its nourishing magnificence.

Betwixt the realms of truth and fantasy
My ego floats in the breeze of ecstasy,
Refusing to admit it a mere deception
Far from the nature of true perception.

Life in a fantasy world is unreal
It must combine with cheer and ordeal,
Twin sides of life's essential nature
Is truly crucial to revel in rapture.

20. A Rustic's Query

The scene was uncanny and weird
For the unread rustic,
Such events had ne'er appeared,
Seemed myth and mystic.

Cloud talking to cloud is absurd,
Rain pelted stones,
Fish swam in circles and cluttered,
Dogs fought for bones.

Leaves slapped each other he knew,
Birds pecked on trees,
Sting of bees is repaid in lieu
Of sweet honey.

His farmland is vast yet uneven
Just hills and vales,
No protection under the moon
When a storm assails.

Such events are beyond his cognition
Hard he may try,
In the absence any sense of ambition
Their existence deny.

21. The Womb is a Mystery

A womb is a sanctuary heaven ordained
To cradle and nurture the human seed,
A floating bed cozy, safe and unfeigned,
Cocooned, cherished and in love confined.

The feelings of delight are purely maternal
That hold the flow of love, slow and even,
Within this eternal receptacle
Amidst pangs of birth mothers live in.

Hugged by a mass of flesh and bones
The womb swaddles a life emerging,
With rising and falling of breathing and groans
Painfully the mother savors the feeling.

The first thing the infant learns is to cry
Not a soft whimper but a loud scream,
He wants to proclaim to the low and the high
That his birth was God's eternal dream.

22. Get Down to Reality

Breezing through a cloud of fluttering feathers
My soul perched on a twig of emotions,
Listening to the cry of unseen creations
Trapped in cages or bound with fetters.

Shadows of phantoms on waves of solitude
Spinning a web of mystical desires
Infused a surreal world that conspires
To project a physical semblance of attitude.

My angst at confronting vagueness of purpose
Explored deeper the core of fantasy
To discern clues hidden pacing aimlessly
That provoked my concern for this futile pose.

Life in this abstract and intangible sphere,
Devoid of substance and shapeless in form
Created distrust that defied the norm,
The change from fancy to matter was severe.

Joe Anthony

F.Discourse with the Divine

Man cannot live on his own. He needs help and support. Every man is designed to depend on *God*. Dependence starts by acknowledging Him as the owner of everything and the controller of every circumstance. Nothing is impossible with God, and everything is within His reach. Man's part is to trust and obey, and His part is to do the rest.

1. God's Spirit

You are the consuming fire
That can't be taught or defined,
Set things ablaze entire
And penetrate the core of our mind.

This fire burns out the dross,
Refines to make us pure gold,
Refills us with your presence,
Illuminates our abode.

You are the water's well spring
The source of our life's essence,
Out of your innermost being
Grace will flow in abundance.

At dawn you're Israel's dew,
Like the lily he'll blossom,
To refresh nature you pursue
And revive and refill his bosom.

Your oil anoints your people,
Consecrates them your own,
Seal them for now and eternal
To keep them by your throne.

Peace, hope and joy are pleasures
Enjoyed when your Spirit arrives,
Your seven gifts are our treasures
That will direct our lives.

2. To the Upper Room

Come with me to the upper room
Let us celebrate the Passover feast,
Though clean, yet I wash your feet
To get you set for the ultimate treat.

"You mustn't do Lord, it's so humbling",
You are our Rabi and we're just pupils",
Wrapped in defects and moral scruples,
Blow flagrantly our faults through bugles.

Here is the choicest meal I've spread
My broken body and my blood too,
Accept as treasures of utmost value
Consume them and life eternal pursue.

Do it for others for they too are in need
Let my self-offering be an example
You too must follow and don my mantle
Become me and proclaim my preamble.

3. The Call was Loud

He heard me call out loud
From deep within my heart,
The reply pierced the cloud
Which split my soul apart.

Eloquent was its impact
Resonated within my depth,
Stirred up the shallow tract
To come to light from stealth.

Fear knocked at my heart,
I was disconcerted,
Trust provided the start,
Hope assistance asserted.

My response was spontaneous
No hesitation persisted,
Smoothly flowed out harmonious
Which heaven accepted.

4. Lay Your Hands

Place your hand on my head
With heavenly blessing,
Remove the evil of dread
I've been experiencing.

Let your spirit enter
To claim me your own,
Be my soul's mentor
My spirit's throne.

Let evil assets discard
Free me again,
And wickedness be barred
At the entrance detain.

So shall my spirit rejoice
And endeavor
To proclaim in loud voice
Yours forever.

5. In Expiation

He needed to expiate a hidden sin
That had been groaning and gnawing within,
His effort to commence the process again
Fell through before he could even begin.

His conscience was a cactus of titanic size,
Its needles offered him means to chastise,
His blood oozing out was no surprise,
And its wetness he didn't despise.

He prayed and fasted hoping to gain
The pardon he had been seeking in vain,
And rid his mind of excessive strain,
And a calm and peaceful status attain.

6. In Constant Contact

You'll find me, Lord, every day and night
By your little shrine in the dim light,
Thank you for letting me with you unite,
Devoutly my prayers I shall recite.

Though body's asleep I feel my heart ache
My spirit beside you is fully awake,
Yearns for your loving food to partake
And plead on bended knees not to forsake.

Bowing before you in silent prayer,
Flawed in nature, though I'm well aware,
Yet relying upon your mercy and care
My loyalty to you I firmly declare.

Sitting beside you I inhale your breath
Embalming my heart even to its depth,
Your soothing whispers offer me strength
Your blessings bring me salubrious health.

All through the night during my sleep
Your parses silently heavenward leap,
Psalms I recite with reverence deep
Abundant are the blessings I reap.

At dawn my spirit surveys the scene
As in a mirror or like on a screen,
Content and relieved, my heart serene,
Is eager to continue the same routine.

7. When You are Low

When you feel lonely look at the cross
The Lord has both his arms outstretched,
"Come to me," He says with infinite force,
"You will always be cared for and refreshed."

When you're crushed under the weight of crime
And fail to move further despite effort,
Cling to His loving hand in time,
He will accept you and offer comfort.

When sins were repeated by fallen nature
When we've reached the point lowest ever,
Betrayed him for a few pieces of silver
He didn't the final blow deliver.

If in such conditions you are delivered
There isn't a reason you won't be heard,
Anything more severe or grave be the deed
He'll always be there to help you proceed.

8. Intimate Talk

Prayer is being one with God.
What you do or think or say
Can be the ideal way to pray
And adore the Divine Lord.

Prayer is the primary axis
On which life should revolve,
The orbit you shouldn't miss
From which you must evolve.

Prayer is the root of existence,
The gentle breeze that unveils
God's concealed countenance,
To admit his will ever prevails.

Prayer penetrates every fence,
Can soften a hardened heart,
Or fortify a crumbling defence,
And hope and trust impart.

Prayer is Jacob's ladder
That bridges man with his God,
With humble and honest candor
Can ascend on his own accord.

Empty all pain and grief,
Struggles, failures and flaws,
Extent your hands for relief,
You won't miss His applause.

9. Before a Sacred Icon

The oil lamp diffused its flare
Flickering across her face
She knelt in fervent prayer,
The Psalter in tender embrace.

The hall was filled with awe,
And feelings of sacred stillness
Profound in celestial flow,
Wrapped everyone in fullness.

Timeless portrayal of devotion,
Echoes with humanity's quest,
A tapestry of communal wisdom,
Insights and musings attest.

She sings in melodious praise,
The assembly joins in chorus,
Thanks is offered in bouquets,
And fragrance in anthems glorious.

10. The Betrayer

The rotting lips of the betrayer
Stamped a blemished scar
On the spotless face of the Master,
And in his heart a mar.

The kiss was a sort of reward
For having been accepted,
Letting him sign the accord
And the wallet in charge selected.

The deafening silence of pain,
Shattered by the roar of deceit,
Throbbed through His uneasy brain
In surrender as He knelt.

He looked at the disloyal man
Steadily and sternly in the face,
He knew from the start his plan
His conduct had revealed a trace.

The night was long in the prison,
The trial and verdict at dawn
Found him guilty of treason,
So a plan of action was drawn.

We too have often betrayed
But for such acts we repented,
Had the deceiver pleaded
The Master would have relented.

11. At His Death

At his body's site
Some women unite,
Kept vigil feeling contrite,
All through the night,
Recalling His plight.

By his body they knelt,
His pain they felt,
Sensed their heart melt,
Revered the cleft,
His blood's outlet.

Gruesome their conduct,
The torture, an insult,
Judgment was unjust,
Decision did disgust,
Anger and regret, the result.

His body they dressed
With fine linen wrapped,
In reverence embalmed,
All emotions suppressed,
Felt themselves blessed.

His body they laid
In a stranger's bed,
Due homage paid,
Ardently they prayed,
For heaven's aid.

12. The Three O'clock Wonder

In the solemn stillness of nights
The earth in darkness cloaked,
When peacefully slumber alights
On creation in dreams engrossed,
We lie listening to the invites
To commune with the divine Lord.

At three in the morning He rose
Conquered death and grave,
It's the time for Him, He knows
To guide, comfort and save,
To guard us from hostile foes
And make us firm and brave.

It was at three He ascended,
His floodgate of mercy unsealed
A deluge of grace descended
On whom His love He revealed,
From all harm to be defended,
Became their protecting shield.

He knows our need of Him now,
To seek for wisdom and guidance
And His Spirit on us endow,
With arms raised in suppliance
Pleading humbly we bow
And place steadfast reliance.

At three He makes us worthy
To feel His love profound,
And in boundless mercy
Be soaked, filled and drowned,
For we shall never be thirsty,
Let grateful praises resound.

13. She Knelt in Prayer

She knelt in prayer in the front pew
Bathed in sunlight filtered through
The stained glass, she saw in the loft
Its vibrant hues the hall permeate.

Shrouded in silence in pensive state
She closed her eyes to concentrate,
Heard a knock on the entrance door,
Though startled she chose to ignore.

The air was charged with tension
A prelude in anticipation
Of a mystery she presumed unravel,
The knock at the door of the chapel.

There was no stranger at the scene
Only the presence of the dean,
The relief restored her fervor
Naught intruded to unnerve her.

14. Awaiting a Response

I walked the path of hope
Holding back my regrets,
Searching for every scope
Of safety from unknown threats.

Tethered to the blotted record
That lay moored in my dock,
Will not reach any accord
But stay a stumbling block.

The goodness of past years,
The spark that dimmed in time,
The resolve without fears,
All turned faces of crime.

Like lonely whispers serene
Echo from cloudy dreams,
My cool fingers glean
Naught but insipid themes.

With sighs of anguished plea,
Frail yet stable and firm,
I wait on bended knee
For heaven my fate confirm.

15. The Ultimate Sacrifice

Nobody can unravel the mystery,
Nor guide anyone with mastery,
To fathom the depth of that grace
Of His ultimate sacrifice.

The Lord made a solemn vow
From the cross on Calvary's brow,
He made the essential oblation
Required for our salvation.

We may consult theologians,
Embark on hallowed grounds,
Pour over erudite theses
To study the sacred species.

We need to experience within
That to God we are akin,
When the sacred words spoken
And his body and blood are taken.

He rests and melts on our tongue,
Permeates our entire being,
We blend to evolve a fusion
Of divinity and human vision.

Experience isn't a feeling
Instead a total revealing
Of God to man His presence
As he penetrates our elements.

One who enters the Mass
Must things mundane surpass
In spirit and in vital essence
With complete trust and reliance.

16. Joseph the Just

Emerging from a background hidden and silent,
Born in a dynasty of royal heritage,
Stands out a carpenter from Nazareth village
As a beacon of hope for a world noncompliant.

Gleaning his life reveals a man of modesty
Gentle in manner, self-effacing by nature,
Profound in holiness, reverential in feature,
Obeying God's law and living in honesty.

Peel away the layers and probe little deeper
To find a man of humble demeanor,
Chaste and just in belief and manner,
Exalted is status as the foster father.

A man of faith in the promptings of the Spirit
Lived a life of sacrifice and forbearance,
In deep recollection and severe penance
That his actions may obtain him merit.

Entrusted with the humanity of his son
Into the care of Joseph the innocent
Who believed in dreams but ever vigilant
To protect his Mary and the Divine One.

17. Do it Before it's Late

My life is like a withered old leaf
Fallen after a stay quite brief,
Detached from the tree of its birth
Into the lap of its mother earth.

It has truly fulfilled its plan
Of breathing out oxygen to serve man,
Providing food and water in abundance,
And for the living a secure existence.

My life's journey to its end has begun,
Much has been done, still some undone,
Time is short, can't further extend,
To finish what's pending I must attend.

Here I linger and slowly proceed
To finish the task I had received,
Lest I hear a voice of reproach
As to my eternal home I approach.

18. Daughter of Phanuel

Anna lost her spouse at a young age,
Since then she wrote her story on a page
In a book of seclusion and self-sacrifice,
Living in the temple, offering her service.

She led a life of silent negation
Serving the Lord with intense passion,
Singing praises or praying in silence,
Reading Scripture to grasp its essence.

Always within the confines of the temple,
Away from people, her life was simple,
Delving deep into the core of heaven
Fasting and pleading for sins be forgiven.

Lighting candles and burning incense,
Kneeling in prayer in divine presence,
Decking the altar with flowers of fragrance,
Reciting Psalms she paid obeisance.

Prophetess of God daughter of Phanuel
Awaited the arrival of Emmanuel,
Day and night she worshipped and prayed
To see the Messiah when he arrived.

On her mission she was persistent
Always be focused was her intent,
She's the paradigm of resolute waiting
Even when the delay seemed unending.

19. Discard All Add-Ons

Man is a living magnet perennial
Drawing to himself things often trivial,
No matter the cost or the weight might be
Possess he must, his mind will decree.

Discard everything in life you've collected,
That looked handy and at random selected
On your pleasure tours around the world,
Things though dear yet no use unfurled.

Drop that demeanor haughty and proud
This mindset will be your binding shroud,
Your weight is a burden your body regrets
A slim physique, the best of your assets.

Do away with every remorse and shame,
Trudge the path to lead you to fame,
Leave behind all the sediments of guilt
You have unwittingly labored and built.

Chip away the edges sharp and hurting,
Smoothen the surface to make it glowing,
Cast aside every negative emotion,
Embrace the feeling of being chosen.

Peel off the ugly skin caging your spirit
Let it soar beyond to heaven inherit,
Wash away ugly stains that will limit
Your entry to heaven with due merit.

You can't be crippled by loss and defeat
For your faith's much stronger than your feet,
So, rise throw down the yoke of despair
Embrace the glory He's wanting to share.

20. Women in the Gospels

God entrusted first to women
Things concerning God's mission,
In history's important tidings
Their role had many rulings.

During his earthly ministry
Women had prestige and dignity,
Those who had been healed
Or from demons freed.

They loved Him and ministered,
Out of their own means supported,
Witnessed His miraculous deeds,
And fulfilled their spiritual needs.

It was a woman who anointed
Jesus' human feet and head,
A woman had urged her partner
To spare an innocent's honor.

Women were the ones who stayed
At the foot of the cross dismayed,
And at the tomb came first
To anoint the body of Christ.

The first to witness his rising
Was entrusted with a bidding
To take the news to his brethren
These were given to women.

Jesus loved and respected
Women and men were trusted
Both were equally honored
With freedom they were rewarded.

21. My Guardian Angel

My angel is unique and special,
His love and protection crucial,
He affirms to him I belong,
Under his wings I'm strong,

Gentle and calm by nature,
Holiness, his prime feature,
Contemplates God's face,
And obtains for me His grace.

His love has no start or end
From birth to death a friend,
You may provoke or hurt
His love he'll always assert.

Day and night he's near
A protector and a messenger,
He never abandons me,
For me he's God's trustee.

22. Totus Tuus – Totally Yours

Night and day I'm at your side
Kneeling, sitting or lying beside,
Deeply absorbed in spiritual union
Privileged to be under your dominion.

The soothing whisper of your breath
Penetrates into my soul's depth,
Your heartbeat resonates within my heart
I feel your presence grace impart.

Your profound sanctity with its fragrance
Permeates gently into my essence,
I'm immersed in your divine grace
And in rapture, my Lord, I embrace.

I've been living a life of devotion
Pouring myself out a worthy oblation,
Hoping to partake your nature benign
And live forever in your abode divine.

23. Silence

I hear silence travel with me
Behind and by my side,
I haven't seen him physically
But his presence abide.

His voice is quiet and even
At dawn and all day,
He shouts at night the loudest
And keeps me awake.

Silence makes me think and act
I'm never tired,
I achieve the best of results
With silence around me.

His message is heard only in silence
So are his feelings expressed,
What he thinks and what he does
Are done when he's silent.

24. Generous to a Fault

Ask for a flower
He gives you a garden,
Request for rain
Accept the deluge,
Beg for a light beam
He floods you in light,
Appeal for a day more
He grants you long life
Beseech forgiveness
He deletes your sins,
Pray for a child
He fills your cradle,
Plead for help
He sends you helpers,
God is generous
Even to a fault
There's no doubt.

25. Step into the Sacred Space

Delve into the epochal messages straight
With an open mind and receptive spirit,
As we unravel the layers of grace,
Step into the heart of the sacred space.

God's in control with unwavering precision,
His love unfailing reveals his decision,
His words breathe life into our dreams,
Not on performance but on our themes.

We turn our trials into testimonies,
Our sorrow and pain into purposes,
Our hope is anchored in his promises,
They help us navigate life's realities.

Inhale the fragrance of his redemption
Offered freely to all through revelation.
Like a beacon piercing through darkness
Let his words be our safety harness.

26. The God of the Impossible

Our God is the Alpha and the Omega
Who embraces a mysterious aura,
He's in the business of doing the unexpected
When our soul is with wounds inflicted.

He meets us at the height of our pain,
Surprising us with the grace to attain
And transform our spiritual perspective
Into accomplishments most effective.

His promise of a divine intervention
Can change everything with right intention,
The path ahead may seem daunting and scary
Obscured by the shadows of uncertainty.

"I'm making a way in the wilderness
And streams for you in the waste's vastness,
Hold on to my hand extended to lead you
Hesitate not, have faith firm and true".

Joe Anthony

G. The Lost Countryside

Countryside is usually used to refer to land outside towns and cities, with fields, wood and farms. It is a non-urban area that has a minor population density, small settlements, and vast farmlands.

We find it difficult to look over a large green field and not feel relaxed, or to walk through some woodland and not feel both inspired and calm. It is a fact that spending time in nature will improve mental health and overall wellbeing.

1. Meeting the Unmet

Arduous was the journey to the past
Through meandering by-lanes,
And fields alive with crops that last
A season with good rains.

A journey exhausting yet rewarding,
The pain of distance overrides
The joy of meeting, with love outpouring,
A permanent link provides.

I surveyed the landscape swept by breeze
And crops heavy with grains,
The past was a true replica of these
On the folded terrains.

I could sense their body odor,
Its nave musky feature,
And the sweat that eased the soil's nature,
In their unique candor.

'Distance makes the heart grow fonder'
Of the missed dear ones,
In the womb of time we will wonder
How they scaled life's rungs.

I hadn't met these progenies before
Their parents were my peers,
With them I could affinity restore
They were the early pioneers.

A hug here, a handshake there,
A kiss to revive the memory,
Dormant feelings were kindled to share
To last an eternity.

2. Familiar People

People with faith deep and sincere
His amazing grace honor and revere,
To his decrees and guidance adhere,
In godliness and virtues persevere.

Worship fervently the Lord Almighty
Falling prostrate or on bended knee,
Attributing to him honor and glory
That's the only way life should ever be.

Regular and unfailing in obligation
Prescribed for us by the Lord of creation,
Instilled in us firmly by inspiration,
The only way to our destination.

3. Recalling the Past

Surveying the dense green cultivation
Of seasonal crops o'er a hilly location,
Brought me memories long left behind.

Foregone years in the flush of youth
When peasants were primitive and uncouth,
Simplicity on our badge was designed.

Flash back of those years is still vivid
Reflecting all values we held rigid,
Now ticks the dormant spirit and mind.

Pleasurable emotions yodeled aloud,
Strumming of heartstrings was avowed
Life was delightful with folk songs refined.

Now crops are replaced by concrete groves,
Space has shrunk and no vegetation grows,
Sadly the state of that scene is defiled.

4. The Village Well

Away from dwellings out in the field,
Having its status partially concealed,
Central to both human and savage
Sits alone this lifeline of the village.

This well had been the supplier of water
Serving every kitchen and the farmer,
Its life is spurred by an electric motor,
Bucket and pulley it isn't a promoter.

Queues of ladies at odd hours
Drawing water for drink or showers
Were unique sights for curious foreigners,
A nasty scenes for the harassed villagers.

The well was a place to air their difference,
Gossip, quarrel or reveal their preference,
This luxury now has been withdrawn
After the village had changes undergone.

5. Those Village Folks

Simple and sober in manner,
With natural and honest behavior,
Their values and ethics reflect
What they hold to their heart.

Uncouth may seem their manners,
Unpolished or rude their answers,
Their environ of non-idyllic style
Is devoid of deceit and guile.

Despite their boorish manner
Deep within there's candor,
Projecting an unkempt façade
Transformed with due regard.

Morning till evening they toil
Often in an unfriendly soil,
Wrestling with drought and heat,
Weary but ne'er accept defeat.

Glad when their labor yields
An abundance from the fields,
A worthy reward to celebrate
And delight and pride generate.

6. The Old Village No More

The old village has turned a mini town,
Mud walls, thatched roofs all taken down,
Reborn with new look, color and shape
Makes an onlooker in wonder gape.

Many dwellings have emerged all over
Competing with each refined neighbor
To acquire a unique and distinct character
That will their name and fame register.

Roads are wide and well maintained,
Footpaths of old have status attained,
Street lights safety and comfort provide,
A new society seems have arrived.

Though it's pleasurable to see around,
And the ambience will everyone astound,
Good old ways are missed and dreamed,
As old customs can't be redeemed.

7. A Epic Reunion

Thunder of wonders, a glorious wonder
Burst upon people I didn't remember,
Lost in the past some decades ago
Yet alive now and still on the go.

As pre-teens we loved the countryside,
Played in alleys narrow or wide,
Climbed every tree and swam in the pond,
Fought and made up to retain our bond.

Old and weak now, yet we've prospered,
Three generations we loved and fostered,
The outcome is an astounding reward
In the saga of our family's record.

We hugged and kissed as never before,
Determined to have the kinship restore,
Revive and stimulate its steady growth,
And avoid any delays or failures loathe.

My youngest brother took the initiative
Drove us through places classy and primitive,
Mounts and valleys didn't alter our goal
For our intent was firmly in control.

Six days unnerved we drove in focus,
Space and time in no way provoked us,
A journey so special, a meeting so tangible
For a lifetime heaven made it feasible.

                                    Joe Anthony

NO	INDEX
1	A BLISSFUL ATMOSPHERE
2	A DEAD HEAP
3	A DIFFERENT HOME
4	A FORCE THAT LEADS
5	A GENUINE BEGGAR
6	A GLASS BOTTLE
7	A MASTER SMUGGLER
8	A MYSTICAL EXPERIENCE
9	A NEW RAINBOW
10	A PROUD SPIRIT
11	A RIPE OLD LEAF
12	A ROMANTIC SCENE
13	A RUSTIC'S QUERY
14	A SINCERE PROMISE
15	A SOUL IN PAIN
16	A TEARDROP
17	A TRAGIC BIRTHDAY
18	A TREASURE TROVE
19	A UNIQUE LANGUAGE
20	A VISI TO AJNA'S SCHOOL
21	A WELCOME DISTURBANCE
22	A WORLD IN TURMOIL
23	AN ACCIDENTAL MEET
24	AN ANCIENT MANUSCRIPT
25	AN EERIE SETTING
26	AN EPIC REUNION
27	AN EVIL GENERATION
28	AN EVIL QUEEN
29	ANXIOUS WAIT

30	AT HIS DEATH
31	AWAITING A RESPONSE
32	BE A SUNBEAM
33	BEAUTIFUL DESERT
34	BEAUTY REVEALED THE TRUTH
35	BEFORE A SACRED ICON
36	BENEATH THE FROZEN TURF
37	BEWARE
38	BEYOND THE SENSES
39	BLIND PERFORMANCE
40	CAGED IN ENIGMAS
41	CAPRICIOUS LOVE
42	CHANGE IN STRATEGY
43	CLEAR AS CRYSTAL
44	CONFRONTING TEASERS
45	CROSSING THE HURDLE
46	DAUGHTER OF PHANUEL
47	DESTINY
48	DIFFUSE THE FRAGRANCE
49	DISCARD ALL ADD-ONS
50	DISCOURSE WITH THE DIVINE
51	DO IT BEFORE IT'S LATE
52	ECHOES OF SPRING
53	EXPERIENCE OF LOVE
54	FAMILIAR PEOPLE
55	FAMILIAR PEOPLE
56	FANCY
57	FAULTY APPROACH
58	FEIGNED LOVE
59	FIGHTING FOR JUSTICE
60	FILIAL LOVE

61	FIRM FOUNDATION
62	FOR A GOOD HARVEST
63	FORSAKEN AND FORLORN
64	GENEROUS TO A FAULT
65	GET DOWN TO REALITY
66	GOD'S SPIRIT
67	HE CONFRONTS THE ORDEAL
68	HE ENTERS UNDETECTED
69	HEALTHY MORNING AIR
70	HER LONELY HOME
71	HER MYSTERIOUS WAYS
72	HER MYSTERIOUS WAYS
73	HIDDEN IN PAIN
74	I FUND THE LOST COUNTRYSIDE
75	I HEARD HIS STILL VOICE
76	IN A FANCY MOOD
77	IN CONSTANT CONTACT
78	IN EMPATHY'S BOSOM
79	IN EXPIATION
80	IN NATURE'S EMBRACE
81	IN THE ARMS OF NIGHT AND DAY
82	IN THE PALM OF PAIN
83	IN THE PURE OF HEART
84	INTERIOR CONFLICT
85	INTIMATE TALK
86	INVEST IN FULLNESS
87	IT KEEPS NO GRUDGE
88	IT'S WORTH THE EFFORT
89	JOSEPH THE JUST
90	LAY YOUR HANDS
91	LIFE EXPERIENCES

92	LIFE IN A GRANITE CHUNK
93	LIFE WITHOUT WORDS
94	LIKE A MAIDEN
95	LIKE THE GRAIN OF WHEAT
96	LOVE ABIDES IN LONGING
97	LOVE BLOOMS IN SACRIFICE
98	LOVE BY FORCE
99	LOVE IN CONCEALED DISTRUST
100	LOVE IN DEATH
101	LOVE IS AN ART
102	LOVE OF A KIND
103	LOVE ON A PLATTER
104	LOVE SWAYS IN THE BREEZE
105	LOVE THROUGH THE SENSES
106	LOVE WITH A PRICE
107	LOVE'S DWELLING PLACE
108	MAKE SPACE WITHIN
109	MAN'S CONCEPT OF LAW
110	MEETING THE UNMET
111	MEMORY
112	MISSING YOU
113	MY BRAIN IS A GRAVE
114	MY CUP IS FULL
115	MY FUTILE SEARCH
116	MY GUARDIAN ANGEL
117	MY INSPIRATION
118	MY LIFE IS A TAPESTRY
119	MY LIFE IS AN EDIFICE
120	MY SONG IS DISTINCT
121	NATURAL BONDING
122	OLD AGE IS BEAUTIFUL

123	ONE WAY LOVE
124	OVERAMBITIOUS
125	PEACE DISPLACED TURMOIL
126	PEEP THROUH CRREATION
127	PEOPLE OF FAITH
128	PILGRIMS OF HOPE
129	PLAIN TRUTH
130	RAVAGES OF HATRED
131	RECALLING THE PASR
132	REST BEFORE THE QUEST
133	REVISITING AJNA
134	SEARCHING FOR LOVE
135	SEEKING SECRETS
136	SHE KNELT IN PRAYER
137	SHE STOOD MOTIONLESS
138	SHE STORMED OUT
139	SHE WAS A CANDLE
140	SHE WAS DIFFERENT
141	SILENCE
142	SNOBBISH ARROGANCE
143	SORROW AND PAIN
144	SOURCE OF WISDOM
145	SPRING TIME
146	STEP INTO THE SACRED SPACE
147	STERILE OUTLOOK
148	SUFFERING AND SALVATION
149	SWIMMING IN A CESSPOOL
150	THE ABIDING LINK
151	THE BETRAYER
152	THE BRIGHTER SIDE
153	THE CALL WAS LOUD

154	THE CIRCLE EFFECT
155	THE CORRUPT LAWYER
156	THE DISCONNECT
157	THE DISOWNED
158	THE ESSENCE OF EXISTENCE
159	THE FACE OF REALITY
160	THE FINAL JOURNEY
161	THE GARDEN WITHIN
162	THE GENOCIDE
163	THE GOD OF THE IMPOSSIBLE
164	THE LOVE WITHIN
165	THE MOUNTAIN RIVER
166	THE NORMAL
167	THE OLD VILLAGE NO MORE
168	THE SEA AND THE SKY
169	THE SPIDER WEB
170	THE THREE O'CLOCK WONDER
171	THE TYRANT SUN
172	THE ULTIMATE SACRIFICE
173	THE UNFAITHFUL
174	THE VILLAGE WELL
175	THE WAY THEY WORK
176	THE WHIRL OF PAIN
177	THE WINTRY WIND
178	THE WOMB IS A MYSTERY
179	THE WOUNDED BIRD
180	THOSE VILLAGE FOLKS
181	THOUGHT- PROVOKING
182	TIME IS A MYSTERY
183	TIME IS DYING
184	TO THE END OF THE EARTH

185	TO THE UPPER ROOM
186	TODAY MY HEART DIED
187	TOTUS TUUS
188	TRANQUILLY WE LIVED
189	TWO LOVING BEES
190	UNDER HIS SHELTER
191	WAITING DEMANDS PATIENCE
192	WE ARE HIS MIRACLES
193	WE ARE LIKE CIRCLES
194	WE COULD BE THEIR RESIDUE
195	WE HOLD THE POWER
196	WE LOVE THE MORROW
197	WE'RE IN AN EVIL ERA
198	WHAT MATTERS MOST
199	WHEN LOVE FLOWERS
200	WHEN LOVE ISN'T LOVE
201	WHEN OLD AGE CREAPS IN
202	WHEN YOU ARE LOW
203	WHERE THERE IS CONCERN
204	WINDS OF CHANGE
205	WITHIN A MOTHER
206	WOMEN IN THE GOSPELS
207	WONDERFUL YOU
208	WORDS ARE TREASURES
209	YOU DISAPPEARED
210	YOU WERE A WELCOME SONG
211	YOUR ELUSIVE SHADOW
212	YOUR EYES BECKONED ME

www.ingramcontent.com/pod-product-compliance
Lightning Source LLC
LaVergne TN
LVHW091629070526
838199LV00044B/991